Letters from Early Mesopotamia

Writings from the Ancient World
Society of Biblical Literature

Volume 3
Letters from Early Mesopotamia
by Piotr Michalowski
Edited by Erica Reiner

Letters from Early Mesopotamia

by
Piotr Michalowski

Edited by
Erica Reiner

Scholars Press
Atlanta, Georgia

The Society of Biblical Literature gratefully acknowledges a grant from the National Endowment for the Humanities to underwrite certain editorial and research expenses of the Writings from the Ancient World series. Published results and interpretations do not necessarily represent the view of the Endowment.

Library of Congress Cataloging-in-Publication Data

Letters from early Mesopotamia / translated by Piotr Michalowski ;
edited by Erica Reiner.
p. cm. — (Writings from the ancient world ; 3)
Translations from Sumerian, Akkadian, and Eblaite.
Includes bibliographical references and index.
ISBN 1-55540-819-2 (cloth). — ISBN 1-55540-820-6 (pbk.)
1. Assyro-Babylonian letters. 2. Sumerian letters. 3. Eblaite letters. 4. Assyro-Babylonian letters—Translations into English. 5. Sumerian letters—Translations into English 6. Eblaite letters—Translations into English. I. Michalowski, Piotr. II. Reiner, Erica, 1926–. III. Series: Writings from the ancient world ; no. 3.
PJ3882.L46 1993
492′.1—dc20 92-43832
CIP

Printed in the United States of America
on acid-free paper.

Contents

Series Editor's Foreword

Writings from the Ancient World (WAW) presents up-to-date, reliable, and felicitous English translations of important documents from the ancient Near East. Covering the period from the beginning of Sumerian civilization to the age of Alexander, WAW tries to meet research needs of specialists while contributing to general education and cultural awareness.

Translators and editors have kept in mind a broad audience that includes, among others, scholars in the humanities for whom convenient access to new and reliable translations will aid comparative work; general readers, educators, and students for whom these materials may help increase awareness of our cultural roots in preclassical civilizations; specialists in particular cultures of the ancient world who may not control the languages of neighboring societies.

The editors envision that over time the series will include collections of myths, epics, poetry, and law codes; historical and diplomatic materials such as treaties and commemorative inscriptions; and letters and commercial documents. Other volumes will offer translations of hymns, prayers, rituals, and other documents of religious practice. The aim is to provide a representative, rather than exhaustive, sample of writings that broadly represent the cultural remains of various ancient civilizations.

The preparation of this volume was supported in part by a generous grant from the Division of Research Programs of the National Endowment for the Humanities. The Society of Biblical Literature also provided significant financial and administrative support. In addition, all scholars involved in preparing this volume received financial and clerical assistance from their respective institutions. Were it not for these expressions of confidence in our intentions, the arduous tasks of preparation, translation, editing, and publication—indeed, planning for the series itself—simply would not have been undertaken.

Piotr Michalowski prepared and translated the original documents, including necessary collations of tablets. He also wrote the introductory and explanatory material. Erica Reiner carefully read and commented on the manuscript and helped correct proofs on behalf of the series.

BURKE O. LONG

Chronological Table

Uruk Period	3500-2800
Early Dynastic Period	2800-2334
Sargonic Dynasty	2334-2154
Sargon	2334-2279
Rimush	2278-2270
Manishtushu	2269-2255
Naram-Sin	2254-2218
Shar-kali-sharri	2217-2193
Other kings	2192-2154
Gutian Period	2153-2111
Third Dynasty of Ur	2112-2004
Ur-Namma	2112-2095
Shulgi	2094-2047
Amar-Sin	2046-2038
Shu-Sin	2037-2029
Ibbi-Sin	2028-2004
First Dynasty of Isin (Early Old Babylonian Period)	2017-1794
Ishbi-Erra	2017-1985
Shu-ilishu	1984-1975
Iddin-Dagan	1974-1954
Ishme-Dagan	1954-1935
Lipit-Ishtar	1934-1924
Other kings	1923-1794

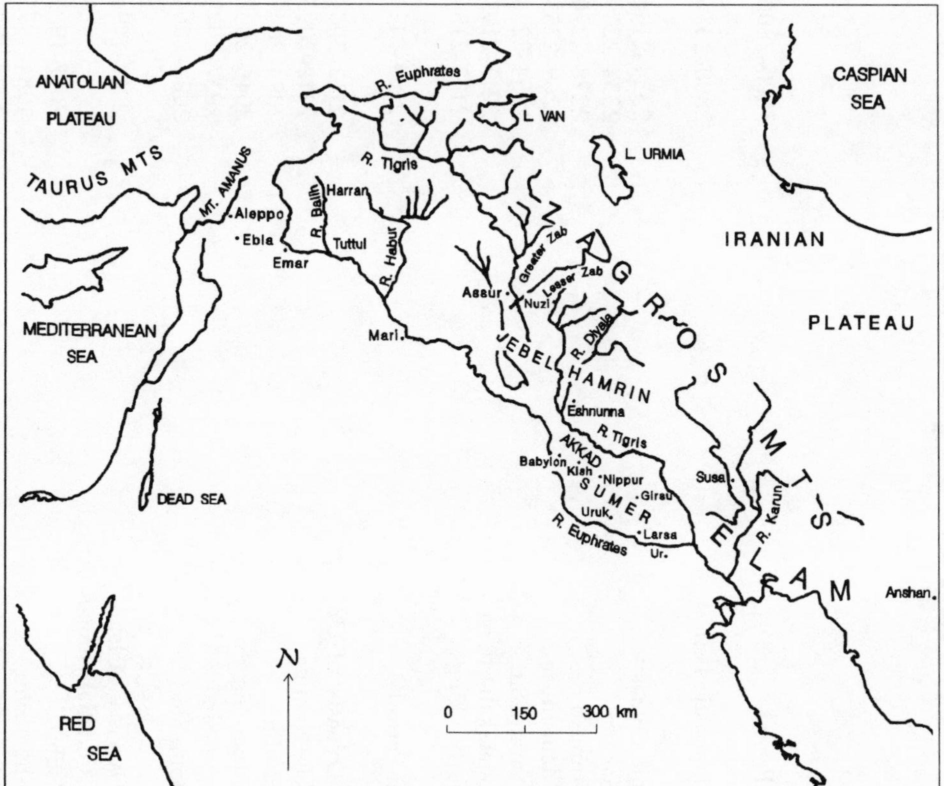

Map of Ancient Near East

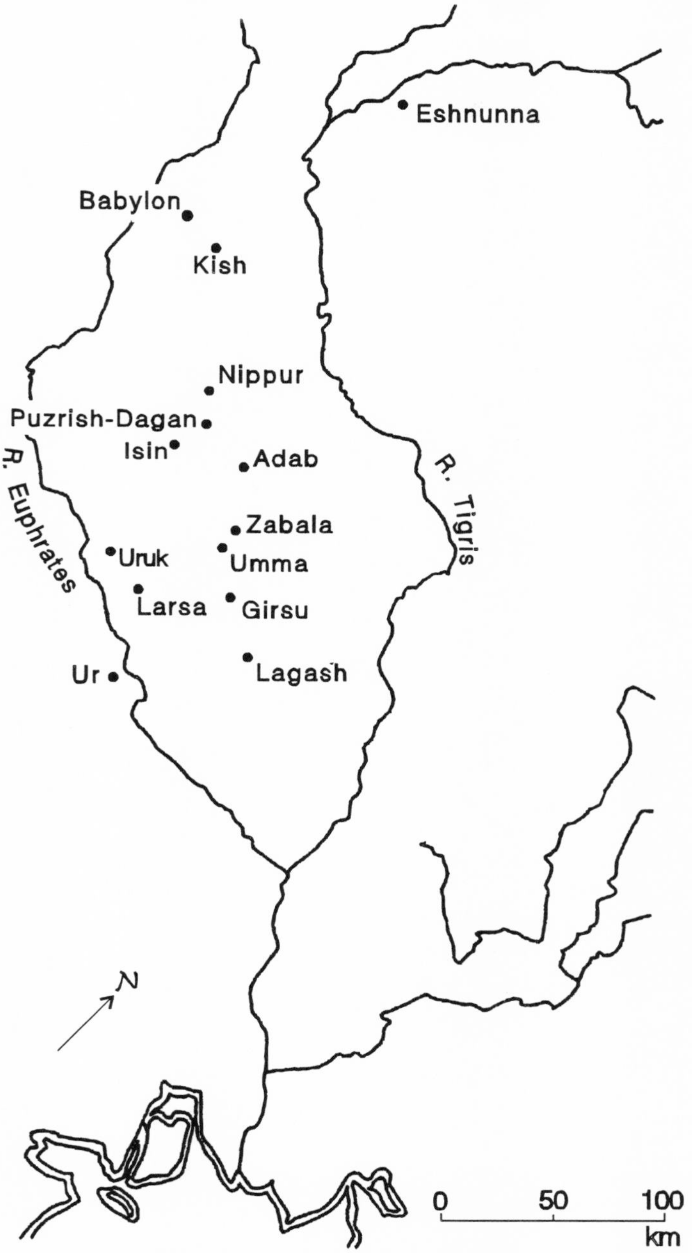

Detail of Southern Mesopotamia

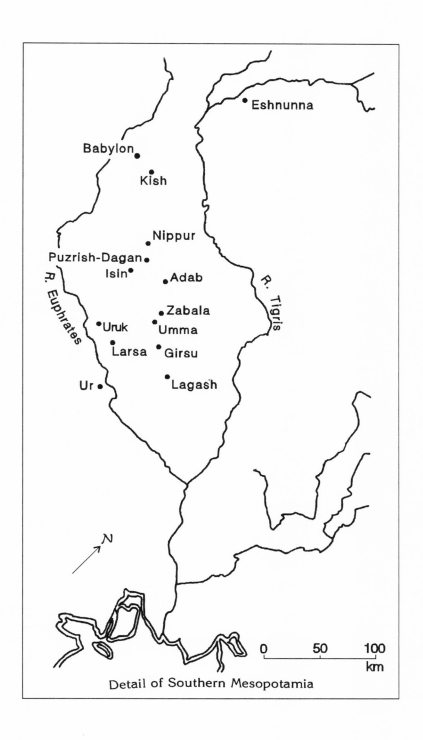

Abbreviations

AOAT	Alter Orient und Altes Testament
AoF	*Altorientalische Forschungen*
AOS	American Oriental Series
ASJ	*Acta Sumerologica (Japan)*
AUCT	Andrews University Cuneiform Texts
BIN	Babylonian Inscriptions in the Collection of J. B. Nies
BM	British Museum, inventory numbers
BO	*Bibliotheca orientalis*
CIRPL	*Corpus des inscriptions "royales" présargoniques de Lagaš* (Sollberger 1956b)
CT	Cuneiform Texts from Babylonian Tablets in the British Museum
DPA	*Étude de documents de la période d'Agadé appartenant à l'Université de Liège* (Limet 1973)
DV	*Dokumenty khoziaistvennoi otchetnosti drevneishei epokhi Khaldei* (Nikol'skii 1915)
Figulla, Catalogue	*Catalogue of the Babylonian Tablets in the British Museum, I* (Figulla 1961)
Gomi–Sato	*Selected Neo-Sumerian Administrative Texts from the British Museum* (Gomi and Sato 1990)
HSS	Harvard Semitic Series
ITT	Inventaire des tablettes de Tello conservées au Musée Impérial Ottoman
JAOS	*Journal of The American Oriental Society*
JCS	*Journal of Cuneiform Studies*
JEOL	*Jaarbericht van het Vooraziatisch-Egyptisch Genootschap "Ex Oriente Lux"*
JRAS	*Journal of the Royal Asiatic Society*
MAD	Materials for the Assyrian Dictionary
M.A.R.I.	*Mari, Annales de recherches interdisciplinaires*
MCS	*Manchester Cuneiform Studies*
MVN	Materiali per il vocabulario neosumerico
Nakahara	*The Sumerian Tablets in the Imperial University of Kyoto* (Nakahara 1928)

NATN *Neo-Sumerian Archival Texts Primarily from Nippur in the University Museum, The Oriental Institute and the Iraq Museum* (Owen 1982a)
NBC Nies Babylonian Collection, Yale University, inventory numbers
Ni Nippur collection, Istanbul Archaeological Museums, inventory numbers
OAIC *Old Akkadian Inscriptions in Chicago Natural History Museum* (Gelb 1955)
OLP *Orientalia lovaniensia periodica*
*Or*NS *Orientalia,* new series
PDT 2 *Die Puzriš-Dagan-Texte der Istanbuler Archäologischen Museen* (Yıldız and Gomi 1988)
RA *Revue d'assyriologie*
RIAA *Recueil des inscriptions de l'Asie Antérieure des Musées Royaux du Cinquantenaire à Bruxelles* (Speleers 1925)
RTC *Recueil de tablettes chaldéennes* (Thureau-Dangin 1903)
STR *Sumerian Temple Records of the Late Ur Dynasty* (Lutz 1928)
STTI *Sargonic Texts from Telloh in the Istanbul Archaeological Museums* (Donbaz and Foster 1982)
TAD *Tablets from the Archives of Drehem* (Langdon 1911)
TCS Texts from Cuneiform Sources
TENUS *Textes économiques néo-sumériens de l'Université de Syracuse* (Sigrist 1983)
TIM Texts in the Iraq Museum
TJAMC *Tablettes juridiques et administratives de la IIIe dynastie d'Ur et de la Ire dynastie de Babylone* (Szlechter 1963)
TLB *Tabulae Cuneiformes a F. M. Th. de Liagre Böhl collectae*
TMH *Texte und Materialen der Frau Professor Hilprecht Collection of Babylonian Antiquities im Eigentum der Universität Jena*
Touzalin, Administration *L'administration palatiale à l'époque de la Troisième Dynastie d'Ur. Textes inédits du musée d'Alep* (Touzalin 1982)
TrDr *La trouvaille de Dréhem* (de Genouillac 1911a)
TSU *Textes sumériens de la IIIe Dynastie d'Ur* (Limet 1976)
TU *Tempelurkunden aus Tello* (Reisner 1901)
U Umma Collection, Istanbul Archaeological Museum, inventory numbers
UDT *Ur Dynasty Tablets* (Nies 1920)
UET *Ur Excavations, Texts*
UIOM University of Illinois, Classical Museum, inventory numbers
USP *Umma in the Sargonic Period* (Foster 1982a)
VDI *Vestnik Drevnei Istorii*
Yang, Adab *Sargonic Inscriptions from Adab* (Yang 1989)
YOS Yale Oriental Series. Babylonian Texts

Explanation of Signs

[ ] Single brackets enclose restorations.

⸢ ⸣ Half brackets enclose partially destroyed signs.

: A colon in the transliterations designates signs in reverse order.

‹ › Angle brackets enclose words omitted by the original scribe.

( ) Parentheses enclose additions in the English translation.

. . . A row of dots indicates gaps in the text or untranslatable words.

PN = personal name

Italics in the English translations indicate uncertain renderings.

Introduction

This volume provides a selection of letters from ancient Western Asia up to the time of the First Dynasty of Isin in Mesopotamia. These letters were written on clay tablets with cuneiform characters; they are the earliest epistolary writings known to us from any part of the globe. The texts are translated from three languages—Sumerian, Eblaite, and Old Akkadian—all of which are imperfectly understood at present. Specialists in these languages will undoubtedly question many of the renditions presented here, as there is not a text in this volume that could not be translated differently. To give the non-specialist reader some sense of the original documents, the translations are accompanied by transliterations of the cuneiform texts.

The first writing system was devised more that five thousand years ago in the land of Sumer, that is, in the southern part of the territory occupied presently by Iraq. The writing, which we call proto-cuneiform, was most probably invented to render the Sumerian language, a tongue that died out thousands of years ago. Sumerian has never been successfully linked with any other language or language family and must be reconstructed solely on internal grounds. Southern Mesopotamia, that is, Sumer, and its northern counterpart, which following ancient usage we call Akkad, was peopled by multicultural and multilingual societies, and eventually the more developed system, which is known as cuneiform (that is, "wedge-shaped") was used as a vehicle for writing several Semitic languages and dialects: Akkadian, Eblaite, and at least one more unidentified member of this language family. This type of writing spread far outside of Mesopotamia proper, and for more than two millennia it was used to express many languages, including Elamite, Hurrian, and Hittite. In the latter part of the second millennium Akkadian became the standard diplomatic language throughout the Near East and even in Egypt.

The first texts were drawn on clay, the most characteristic material of a landscape deprived of wood and stone. The choice of material was fortunate for modern investigators of the past. The baked or sun-dried clay tablets, used for over three thousand years, survived the local climate in the millions, and historians continue to be deluged by new information almost on a daily basis as the ruins of the Near East—and the storerooms of modern museums—reveal more and more of these remnants of ancient cultures.

The earliest known texts are administrative documents; mixed with them almost from the beginning are lists of words that were used to teach the skill to the next generation of bureaucrats. The earliest tablets are conventionally dated to approximately 3100 BCE. Literary texts are not found until three hundred years later, at least nine generations after the first writings known to us. There is not a single epistolary text among the earliest documents. The first dated letter—and the first example translated below—was composed sometime around the year 2350 BCE, at least 750 years after the invention of writing.

The relatively late appearance of letters is paradoxical. If the purpose of writing is to bridge communicative distance and supplement human memory, then the letter would seem to be the ideal form of this new technology, and yet this genre comes relatively late in the development of written forms of expression. It is instructive that the native Mesopotamian tradition associated the birth of writing with the invention of the letter. Two stories relate this invention; both are written in Sumerian and are preserved on tablets dating to the eighteenth century BCE.

The first story (the modern title is *Enmerkar and the Lord of Aratta*) forms part of a long poetic tale about Enmerkar, a legendary third-millennium king of the city of Uruk. However, the composition dates back no further than 2000 BCE. The central narrative concerns competition over control of trade between two cities that were quite distant from each other: Uruk in southern Iraq (Sumer) and the legendary trading center of Aratta in Iran. The conflict between the two city-states was engaged by means of riddles that were exchanged between the rulers of the two cities. A messenger had to range back and forth between Uruk and Aratta carrying in his memory the arguments of the two rulers. The exchanges became longer and longer; at a certain point we read (Cohen 1973: 136-37; Vanstiphout 1988: 159):

> Because the messenger was heavy of mouth and could not repeat it (the message), Enmerkar, the ruler of Kullaba, patted the clay and wrote words on it as if it were a tablet. At that time writing on clay did not exist but now, as a result, when day broke, thus it was. Enmerkar wrote words on clay, as if on a tablet, thus it was.

The ambassador flew over seven mountain ranges like a bird, arrived at Aratta, and repeated his king's message. He showed the tablet to the local king and then:

> The ruler of Aratta took it from the messenger next to a brazier. The ruler of Aratta looked at the clay, the words were merely wedges, his face darkened (with anger)! The (confounded) ruler of Aratta continued to look at it (in the light of) the brazier!

The only other similar Sumerian story is clearly related. The surviving narrative is part of an incomplete tale about the late third millennium king, Sargon of Akkad (2334–2279 BCE). Before he became the founder of a new dynasty, Sargon, according to native tradition, was a cupbearer at the court of Ur-Zababa, the ruler of the northern Mesopotamian city-state of Kish. The older king had premonitions about his servant and sent him off on an errand to Uruk, to the court of king Lugalzagesi, who reigned later than Enmerkar, the hero of the previous story. In this case all the protagonists are historical figures, although the text was again composed much later. The tale has a familiar ring, albeit with a sinister twist, and it is interesting to compare it with similar later stories from other cultures (Alster 1987):

> At that time writing on tablets indeed existed but enclosing them in clay (envelopes) had not yet been invented. King Ur-Zababa, for Sargon, creature of the gods, wrote a tablet that would cause his own (the bearers') death. He dispatched it to (king) Lugalzagesi in Uruk (Cooper and Heimpel 1982: 77).

These two passages demonstrate that the letter held a privileged place in Mesopotamian discussions of writing. The idea that a letter could kill its bearer is indicative of the ideological danger of written communication: letters can be falsified, altered, or simply lost. One suspects that the composers of the two passages cited above had in mind more complex exchanges than the ones presented in this volume.

It is difficult to establish who wrote the early letters. One could enumerate the professions of the persons and the subject matter that is the substance of the epistles, but this would only answer some of the questions we have. These questions often are phrased in terms of a dichotomy between "written" and "oral," but the issue does not concern specific types of discourse; it is linked with the control and use of literacy. Letters, like administrative documents, were often dictated rather than physically "written" by their authors. Hence, they were filtered through various epistolary conventions, as the small space of the cuneiform tablet required that a long message be reduced to a minimal text. Even those who could write probably used scribes for much of the everyday administrative work. These scribes were authorized to stand in as "authors" in the place of the persons whom they represented. For example, one can demonstrate that there were multiple seals of the governor of the city of Umma during the Ur III period. In this case it is clear that more than one bureaucrat was authorized to seal tablets in the name of the governor; one may assume that similar scenarios have to be reconstructed in other situations.

The early forms of address in letters reflect conventions of dictation and recitation. Since these were standardized, they were used by those who composed their own texts on clay, as well as by those who had others write for them. The earliest form of address contains an imperative verb: "Speak!"

The various address formulas that developed through the centuries retained this imperative mode and suggest the scenario of a scribe writing a letter on orders from a client or master, a messenger carrying the letters to their destination, and either that messenger or someone else reading the missive aloud to the addressee. One cannot rule out, of course, that some officials and men, or women, of affairs could, and would, read and write their own letters, but we have no way of establishing the actual actions of epistolary exchanges. It must be kept in mind that the large majority of early Mesopotamian letters circulated within the sphere of official bureaucratic practice; one looks in vain for intimate private communications, such as those found in later Mesopotamian correspondence. Every now and then a personal note is embedded in the letter, as in text 43 below, but as a rule these are documents from economic archives, and not private missives. This is particularly true of the Ur III letters, which are largely "letter-orders," that is, orders to subordinates in an official chain of command. One could even argue that these texts should not be edited or translated separately, as a pseudo-genre, but that they should be presented together with other types of archival materials that were part of the process of recording various stages of official transactions. Letters 121–24, with their corresponding receipt envelopes, provide some illustration of such recording practices. Ideally, archival letters should be analyzed as elements of archives, and not as discrete generic types.

The archival letters were used in everyday transactions. Since the scribes had to learn how to compose such texts, practice letters quickly gave birth to the literary epistle. This was to happen time and again in literary history; indeed, it is impossible to distinguish between "real" and "imaginary" letters. This is true for Sumerian "literary" letters as well as for classical Greek or Renaissance epistles (Guillén 1986: 85). As early as the Old Babylonian period, letters of Ur III scribes and officials from Nippur and Ur were copied and recopied by students as writing and rhetorical exercises (Hallo 1981). In addition, revised versions of almost thirty letters between Ur III kings and their high military officers were studied in the schools, as were a few letters from the early rulers of Isin. Not a single Ur III original of this correspondence has survived, and if these texts are copies of authentic texts, then one has to assume that the orthography of the letters had been revised to conform with later standards, as there are no surviving traces of earlier writing habits. Although it is possible that all of these texts were fictitious, it is more probable that the core of this royal correspondence was based on actual archival texts, but revised, and that other texts of the same type were written long after the death of the kings of Ur (Michalowski 1976b, 1981). We have no way of unraveling the levels of authenticity, and one could argue that any attempt to do so would be technically impossible, as well as theoretically futile.

In addition to the political letters of earlier kings, the Old Babylonian pupils studied another type of epistle: the poetic letter of petition or, as Assyriologists call it, the letter-prayer (Hallo 1968). The earliest poetic epistles were ascribed to the time of Shulgi, the second ruler of the Ur III dynasty (2094–2047 BCE). Some of them were directed from officials to the king, but the majority were addressed to deities from kings, princesses, scribes, and elite members of society. The complex Sumerian poetic epistles contrast sharply with the simple Akkadian prose letters with similar purpose. It is characteristic that the Sumerian examples are found in numerous copies, because they were school exercises. All the known Akkadian letters of petition addressed to deities are attested in single examples and were written with the same archival hand that was used to write contemporary business letters and documents, not in literary script. The literary letters deserve separate treatment and are not included here, with the exception of two letters exchanged by King Shulgi and his vizier (numbers 96 and 97).

There is some evidence that letter-prayers were placed directly before the cult statue in a temple. How the gods answered is less certain, but we do have a small group of Old Babylonian Akkadian letters addressed from the goddess Ishtar to the head administrator of her temple in the city of Nerebtum (Ellis 1987). It is not certain if this is a local tradition or a remnant of a more widespread practice.

Some observations on the translations are in order. The purpose of this volume is to provide readable English renditions of the letters without violence to the original text. This is not a standard edition, and the transliterations of the Sumerian, Akkadian, and Eblaite originals are intended to give some idea of the problems that a philologist has to face when working with these materials. They are also included to make it easier for those who know the original languages to understand the logic behind the translations. The general reader should keep in mind the difficulties one has to face when dealing with this material. Tablets are often broken; old publications are out of date; our knowledge of the ancient languages, particularly of Eblaite and Sumerian, is still less than perfect; and there are major disagreements between scholars on the proper translations of many ancient words—not to mention arguments about the grammar of the old languages. In a series such as this there is no place for polemic, justification of new interpretations, or discussion of multiple translation possibilities for any given word or passage.

The texts are listed according to the original publication of the hand copy, wherever that is possible, or by first edition. For this I have used the standard Assyriological abbreviations, as this information will only have meaning for specialists. The editions and translations are listed below under "Sources."

The choice of texts was dictated primarily by state of preservation. Small fragments were excluded, although some broken letters were translated to provide the reader with an indication of the problems faced by historians. Texts that required extensive commentary in order to justify novel translations were also kept out of this volume. Since no modern edition of the Early Dynastic and Sargonic letters exists, I have included a good portion of the well-preserved examples. All the Ur III letters published up to 1966 were edited in Edmond

Sollberger's classic *Business and Administrative Correspondence under the Kings of Ur* (TCS 1) and are referred to by the number assigned in that volume. In view of the repetitive nature of many of these texts, I have included a judicious selection of the texts edited by Sollberger, as well as a large portion of the Ur III correspondence that has been made available since his book appeared. Most of these new texts have been published only as drawings of the tablets, what Assyriologists call hand copies, and are translated here for the first time.

The reader should be aware of certain conventions that are used in editions of Sumerian and Akkadian texts. The transliterations represent a conventional rendering in the roman alphabet of the signs of the cuneiform script. Cuneiform writing, as it was applied to the Sumerian language, rendered individual morphemes, including word roots, syllables, and semantic classifiers—that is, words that were not pronounced but were used to help the reader by designating the class of a noun. The same system was adapted to various Semitic languages, including Akkadian and Eblaite. In the periods covered here, the writings consisted primarily of syllabic signs. The standard convention requires that we render the transliterations of these Semitic languages in italics. Sometimes a sign was used to express a whole Sumerian word, although it was read out in Semitic in the appropriate grammatical form. These words are rendered in upper case letters. There are also instances where the reading of a sign is uncertain; these are also transliterated in upper case, although in the translations a conventional reading is used. A good example of this is the name ur-^{d}ba-Ú. The four signs consist of ur, possibly an old Sumerian pronominal element, the semantic classifier DINGIR, "deity," transliterated with a raised letter d, which alerts the reader that what follows is a divine name, the syllable ba, and, finally, Ú, which may have been read as /u/, /wa/, or /ba/. In the translations this is written simply as Ur-Ba'u. Names such as this—"*The one* of (the goddess) Ba'u," are important; most ancient names were short phrases or sentences that had meaning for their bearers and for their contemporaries. Some names were little sentences or phrases, others were simple nouns, such as ka_5, "Fox." Kings sometimes acquired throne names and were careful in the naming of their children. Thus the founder of the Old Akkadian dynasty called himself Sharru-ken, "True King," and his grandson was Shar-kali-sharri, "King of all Kings." The large majority of names are transliterated in this fashion, with hyphens separating the discrete elements. Sometimes, as is the case with Sharru-ken, there already exists a garbled English rendering—in this case Sargon, which came into our language from the Old Testament. One should also note that the farther one moves back in history, the shakier our dating system becomes. All the dates used here are conventional and correspond to the system established by J. A. Brinkman in Oppenheim (1977: 335–48).

The complicated metrological systems in use in these early texts have been rendered into English in a variety of ways. Most measures are provided with customary translations such as "mina" and "shekel," and these are explained in the glossary. The complex volume measures have been reduced to the smallest unit, Sumerian sìla, roughly equivalent to a modern liter. Readers who are interested in this subject can now consult the excellent presentation of all the Mesopotamian metrological systems by Marvin Powell (1989–1990).

Finally, some acknowledgments are in order. Piotr Steinkeller kindly read the manuscript and offered valuable learned comments. Unpublished texts are utilized by permission of the Trustees of the British Museum. I wish to express my gratitude to Brian Keck, who prepared the indexes. I must also thank Gary Beckman, Irving Finkel, Markham Geller, Ulla Kasten, Peter Machinist, Steve Tinney, and Christopher Walker, for collations, bibliographical assistance, and hospitality during the preparation of this volume.

Translations

I

Early Dynastic Letters

An Early Dynastic Letter from Girsu

This is the oldest Mesopotamian letter that can be dated with any degree of accuracy. The addressee, Enetarzi, was the chief administrator of the central temple of the Lagash state, the shrine of the god Ningirsu in Girsu. For many years it was thought that he held this post during the reign of King Enanatum II (c. 2390 BCE), and eventually succeeded him on the throne. There are good reasons for dating this letter to a later time (K. Volk, apud Seltz 1991: 36-37), probably during the reign of Urukagina (c. 2350 BCE).

1. CIRPL 46
(Thureau-Dangin, *RA* 6:139)
(Sumerian)

1. lú-en-na
2. sanga ^{d}nin-mar^{ki}-ka-ke$_4$
3. na-e-a
4. [e]n-e-tar-zi
5. [sanga] ⌜^{d}⌝nin-[gír]-su-ra
6. [du$_{11}$]-ga-⌜na⌝
7. 600 ⌜lú⌝ elam^{ki}
8. lagaš^{ki}-ta
9. níg-gur$_{11}$ elam^{ki}-šè ì-íl
10. lú-en-na
11. san[ga]
12. [^{d}nin-mar^{ki}-ka-ke$_4^{?}$]
13. [lú elam^{ki}-ma]-ka
14. dam-ḫa-ra
15. e-da-ak
16. elam-ma GÍN.KÁR bi-sì
17. 540 elam [. . .]
18. [. . .]
19. 1 ur-[^{d}]ba-Ú
20. lú DUN-⌜a⌝
21. níg-lú-nu-DU
22. ugula si[mug]-k[a . . .]
23. šà-b[a] mu-x [. .]
24. é ⌜^{d}nin-mar⌝[^{ki}]-ka-ka ì-dab$_5$

25. 5 zabar kù luḫ-ḫa
26. 20 [. . .]
27. [. . .]
28. [. . .]
29. 5 túg nam-lugal
30. 16 síg udu gu$_7$-a bar udu
31. ⸢e⸣-šè-x
32. [. . .]
33. x x [. . .]
34. énsi lagaš^{ki}
35. ti-la-na
36. en-an-na-túm-sipa-zi
37. agrig
38. ti-[la]-n[a]
39. [. . .]
40. n[íg]-du$_7$-na-bi
41. ^{d}nin-mar^{ki}-ra
42. ḫa-⸢mu⸣-na-tùm (year) 5

To Enetarzi, the temple administrator of (the god) Ningirsu, speak: Thus says Lu-enna, the temple administrator of (the goddess) Ninmar:

600 Elamites carried off (plundered) goods from Lagash toward Elam. Lu-enna, the temple administrator of (the goddess) Ninmar did battle in [x] and defeated the Elamites. He [captured/killed] 540 Elamites. Ur-Ba'u, the subordinate of Nig-lunutum, the chief of the smiths . . . in . . . he captured in the temple of Ninmar. He [*retriev*]*ed* five mirrors of washed silver, 20 . . . , . . . , five royal garments, (and) 16 fleeces from *sheep that had been eaten (by the enemy)*.

As long as the ruler of Lagash is alive, as long as Enanatum-sipa-zi, the steward, is alive . . . shall bring . . . to (the goddess) Ninmar. Year 5.

Letters from Ebla

In 1972 an Italian expedition that had been excavating for over a decade at the Syrian site of Tell Mardikh discovered a large archive of cuneiform tablets from the third millennium. Eventually they were able to recover over 1,200 tablets and fragments from four different archives from a large palace. On the basis of an inscribed statue found earlier, it was possible to establish that Tell Mardikh was the site of ancient Ebla, a city known from Mesopotamian, Syrian, and Anatolian sources. The majority of the tablets were inscribed in a new Semitic language, which was immediately named Eblaite. Some scholars believe that this was not the native tongue of the place, but a scribal language brought in from the outside together with the writing system. Literary texts and scribal exercises were also found in the main archive, written in Sumerian, Akkadian, and perhaps in another Semitic language. The dating of the tablets has been a matter of dispute. Today most scholars agree that they are slightly older than the time of Sargon in Mesopotamia.

The majority of the Ebla tablets are administrative receipts, but among them are some sixty or seventy tablets that may perhaps be characterized as letters. Two such texts stand out: a stylized agreement between the rulers of Ebla and the land of Hamazi, and a report from King 'Enna-Dagan of Mari. There is some question whether one should classify these text as letters, but they are included here for comparative purposes.

2. The Hamazi Letter (Eblaite)

This letter was addressed by Ibubu, a high official at the court of Ebla, to an envoy of the ruler of Hamazi, which remains to be located. The letter concerns the exchange of equids for chariots that cemented an alliance between the king of Ebla, Jirkab-Damu, and Zizi, the ruler of Hamazi.

Column i

1. *en-ma*
2. i-bù-bu$_6$
3. AGRIG
4. É
5. EN
6. *'a$_x$*(NI)-*na*
7. SUKKAL.DU$_8$
8. *an-tá*
9. ŠEŠ
10. *ù*
11. *an-na*
12. ŠEŠ

Column ii

1. LÚ.ŠEŠ
2. *mi-nu-ma*
3. AL$_6$.DU$_{11}$.GA
4. *ze*
5. KA
6. *an-na*
7. IN.NA.ŠÚM
8. *ù*

Column iii

1. *an-tá*
2. AL$_6$.DU$_{11}$.GA
3. *ze*
4. Ì.NA.ŠÚM
5. BAR.AN SA$_6$
6. ḪI.MU.TÙM
7. *an-tá*
8. ŠEŠ
9. *ù*
10. *an-na*
11. ŠEŠ

Column iv

1. 10 ^{giš}ÉŠ
2. 2 ^{giš}GAM ^{giš}TASKARIN
3. i-bù-bu$_6$
4. IN.NA.ŠÚM
5. SUKKAL.DU$_8$
6. ìr-kab-da-mu
7. EN
8. eb-la^{ki}
9. ŠEŠ
10. zi-zi
11. EN
12. ḫa-ma-zi-im^{ki}

Column v

1. zi-zi
2. EN
3. ḫa-ma-zi-im^{ki}
4. ŠEŠ
5. ìr-kab-da-mu
6. EN

Column vi

1. eb-la^{ki}
2. *ù*
3. ti-ra-il
4. DUB.SAR
5. GÁL.TAG$_4$
6. *'a$_x$*(NI)-*na*
7. SUKKAL.DU$_8$

Column vii

1. Ì.NA.ŠÚM

Thus (says) Ibubu, the steward of the palace of the king to the envoy: I am (your) brother and you are (my) brother. What is (appropriate) to brother(s): whatever desire you express, I shall grant and you, (whatever) desire (I express), you shall grant.

May you deliver to me the finest quality equids. You are (my) brother and I am (your) brother. (Therefore I), Ibubu, have given (you), the envoy, ten (wagon) ropes, and two boxwood wagons.

Jirkab-Damu, the king of Ebla is the brother of Zizi, the king of Hamazi; Zizi, the king of Hamazi, is the brother of Jirkab-Damu, king of Ebla.

Jirkab-Damu, the king of Ebla, and the scribe Tira-il have *dispatched* (the goods) to the envoy.

3. The 'Enna-Dagan Letter (Eblaite)

The letter of 'Enna-Dagan, a ruler of Mari, to the king of Ebla, has been the subject of much debate since it was published by Giovanni Pettinato (1980). It was first interpreted as a missive from an Eblaite general who had conquered Mari and surrounding cities. In a new edition of the text, D. O. Edzard (1981) proposed that 'Enna-Dagan was an independent ruler of Mari and that the letter recounted his own military exploits, as well as those of his predecessors on the throne. The text is repetitive and difficult to understand; the translation proposed here is highly tentative. Particularly difficult are the verbs that are rendered here as "defeat," and "pile up burial mounds."

Obverse

Column i

1. *en-ma*
2. en-na-da-gan
3. EN
4. ma-rí^{ki}
5. ʾa$_x$(NI)-*na*
6. EN
7. eb-la^{ki}
8. a-bù-ru$_{12}$^{ki}
9. *ù*
10. ⸢íl⸣-gi^{ki}
11. KALAM^{tim}.KALAM^{tim}
12. be-la-an^{ki}

Column ii

1. sá-ù-mu
2. EN
3. ma-rí^{ki}
4. GÍN.ŠÈ
5. DU$_6$ KIRI$_6$
6. *in*
7. KUR^{ki}
8. la-ba-na-an
9. GAR
10. ti-ba-la-at^{ki}
11. *ù*
12. íl-wi-ì^{ki}
13. sá-ù-mu

Column iii

1. EN
2. ma-rí^{ki}
3. GÍN.ŠÈ
4. *in*
5. KUR^{ki}
6. an-ga-i-[?]
7. DU$_6$ [KIRI$_6$]
8. GAR
9. KALAM^{tim}.KALAM^{tim}
10. ra-ʾà-ak^{ki}
11. *ù*
12. ni-rúm^{ki}
13. *ù*
14. áš-al-du^{ki}
15. *ù*

Column iv

1. ba-dul^{ki}
2. [sá]-⸢ù⸣-mu
3. EN
4. ma-rí^{ki}
5. GÍN.ŠÈ
6. *in*
7. ZAG
8. [x]-an
9. *in*
10. na-ḫal
11. DU$_6$ KIRI$_6$
12. GAR
13. *ù*
14. ì-mar^{ki}
15. *ù*
16. la-la-ni-um^{ki}
17. *ù*

Column v

1. *ga-nu-um*
2. eb-la^{ki}
3. iš-tup-šar
4. LUGAL
5. ma-rí^{ki}
6. GÍN.ŠÈ
7. *in*
8. ì-⸢mar⸣^{ki}
9. *ù*
10. *in*
11. la-la-ni-um^{ki}
12. DU$_6$ KIRI$_6$
13. GAR
14. *ù*
15. ga-la-la-bí-ì^{ki}
16. [*ù*]

Column vi

1. [. . .]^{ki}
2. ⸢*ù*⸣
3. *ga-nu-um*
4. ŠU.DU$_8$
5. ib-lul-il
6. EN
7. ma-rí^{ki}
8. *ù*
9. A.BAR.SAL^{ki}
10. GÍN.ŠÈ
11. *in*
12. za-ḫi-ra-an
13. *ù*
14. ⸢7⸣ DU$_6$ KIRI$_6$
15. [. . .]

Column vii

1. GAR
2. ib-lul-il
3. EN
4. ma-rí^{ki}
5. *ù*
6. ša-da$_5$^{ki}
7. *ù*
8. ad-da-li-ì^{ki}
9. *ù*
10. a-rí-šúm^{ki}
11. KALAM^{tim}.KALAM^{tim}
12. bur-ma-an^{ki}
13. LÚ
14. su-gú-rúm^{ki}
15. ib-lul-il

Column viii

1. GÍN.ŠÈ
2. *ù*
3. DU$_6$ KIRI$_6$
4. GAR
5. *ù*
6. ša-ra-an^{ki}
7. *ù*
8. dam-mi-um^{ki}
9. ib-lul-il
10. LUGAL
11. ma-rí^{ki}
12. GÍN.ŠÈ
13. 2 DU$_6$ KIRI$_6$
14. GAR

Column ix

1. *in*
2. ne-ra-at^{ki}
3. *ù*
4. *in*

5. É.NA
6. ḫa-zu-wa-an^{ki}
7. È
8. ib-lul-il
9. LUGAL
10. ma-rí^{ki}
11. *ù*
12. MU.DE$_6$
13. eb-la^{ki}

Reverse

Column i

1. ŠÀ-*sù*
2. NE-má^{ki}
3. ŠU BA$_4$.TI
4. *ù*
5. ì-mar^{ki}
6. ÍB × SAL
7. DU$_6$ KIRI$_6$
8. GAR
9. ib-lul-il
10. LUGAL
11. ma-rí^{ki}
12. *ù*
13. na-ḫal‹ki›
14. [*ù*]

Column ii

1. nu-ba-at^{ki}
2. *ù*
3. ša-da$_5$^{ki}
4. KALAM^{tim}.KALAM^{tim}
5. ga-sùr^{ki}
6. GÍN.ŠÉ
7. *in*
8. ga-na-ne^{ki}
9. *ù*
10. 7 DU$_6$ KIRI$_6$
11. GAR
12. ib-lul-il
13. LUGAL

Column iii

1. ma-rí^{ki}
2. *ù*
3. ba-ra-ma^{ki} MIN
4. *ù*
5. a-bù-ru$_{12}$^{ki}
6. *ù*
7. ti-ba-la-at^{ki}
8. KALAM^{tim}.KALAM^{tim}
9. [b]e-la-an^{ki}
10. GÍN.ŠÈ
11. en-na-da-gan
12. EN
13. ma-rí^{ki}

Column iv

1. [DU$_6$ KIRI$_6$]
2. GAR
3. ma-da-a
4. *in*
5. Ì.GIŠ
6. KALAM^{tim}.KALAM^{tim}
7. ŠU DU$_8$
8. [. . .] x [. . .] x
9. [. . .]
10. [. . .]

11. ib-lul-il
12. LUGAL
13. ma-rí^{ki}
14. [. . .]

Column v

1. [. . .]
2. *si-na-at*

Thus (says) 'Enna-Dagan, the ruler of Mari, to the ruler of Ebla: Sha''umu, king of Mari, defeated (the cities of) Aburu and Ilgi, territories (that were under the rule of) Belan, and heaped up a burial mound in the mountain land of Labanan.

Sha''umu, king of Mari, defeated (the cities of) Tibilat and Ilwi, and heaped up a burial mound in the mountain land of Angai.

Sha''umu, king of Mari, defeated the territories (belonging to the cities of) Ra'ak, Nirum, Ash'aldu, and Badul, and heaped up a burial mound at the border of . . . in *Nahal.*

Then Jishtup-shar, king of Ebla, defeated (the cities of) Emar, Lalanium, and the *ganum* of Ebla, and heaped up burial mound(s) in Emar and Lalanium.

Then Jiblul-il, the king of Ebla and Abarsal, defeated (the cities of) Gala-labi, . . . , and the *Ganum of the Captives,* and heaped up seven burial mounds in (the city of) Zahiran.

After Jiblul-il, king of Mari, had defeated (the cities of) Shada, Addali, and Arishum, territories (that were under the rule of the city of) Burman, which (was under the rule of the city of) Sugurum, and heaped up burial mound(s), then did Jiblul-il, king of Mari, defeat (the cities of) Sharan and Dammium, and heaped up two burial mounds.

Then Jiblul-il, king of Mari, left (the city of) Nerat, and the *fortress* of Hazuwan, and received the tribute due Ebla from the (city of) Nema. He . . . (the city of) Emar, and piled up a burial mound.

Then Jiblul-il, king of Mari, defeated (the troops of) *Nahal,* Nubat, and Shada, territories (ruled by the city of) Gasur, in (the town of) Ganane, and heaped up seven burial mounds.

Then Jiblul-il, king of Mari, defeated Barama, *for the second time,* as well as Aburu and Tibalat, (all belonging to) the territories (ruled by the city of) Belan.

Then 'Enna-Dagan, ruler of Mari, . . . took oil . . . the territories . . .

II

Letters from the Sargonic Period

Early third-millennium attempts to create larger political units in southern Mesopotamia left little trace in the historical record. A larger polity may have existed farther north, centered on the city of Kish, but very little in the way of written documentation has survived from the area. Around 2330 BCE a king of the Sumerian city of Uruk by the name of Lugalzagesi managed to take control of most of the south, but his hegemony was short-lived; he in turn was defeated by Sargon, a new ruler from the north. Sargon, whose name means "Rightful King" in Akkadian, came from the city of Akkad. The location of his capital remains unknown to this day. We know nothing of his previous career. Later tradition has it that he was a cupbearer at the court of Kish who rose to kingship, founded a new city named Akkad, and conquered most of the known world. Whatever his origins, he and his descendants ruled Mesopotamia for over a century, created the first known multinational empire in history, and established many of the native traditions of kingship. The Sargonid kings were revered in later Mesopotamian literature and historiography; their inscriptions were copied and studied by later generations, and fictional texts were composed about their deeds.

Sargon and his family created a highly organized state, together with a new form of hierarchical bureaucracy, and a centralized government concentrated around a charismatic king. His grandson Naram-Sin (2254–2218 BCE) introduced the concept of divine kingship to further strengthen the ideology of the center. New forms of government required new bureaucratic ideas, and centralized schooling of officials resulted in the introduction of the Akkadian language—or rather of its oldest known set of dialects, which we call Old Akkadian—as the language of literature and administration. Akkadian had presumably been the normal language of writing in the north prior to the rise of the Akkad state, but now it was used in the south alongside the older Sumerian tongue.

Sargonic Letters from Girsu

The city of Girsu, modern Tello, was one of the largest and most powerful polities in the later part of the Early Dynastic period and became the capital of a major province in the Sargonic state. It is also the place where Sumerian culture was rediscovered in the nineteenth century. The French vice-consul in Basra, Ernest de Sarzec, conducted eleven seasons of excavations on the mound between 1877 and 1901. After his death, the work continued under Leon Heuzey and Gaston Cross until the outbreak of World War I made it impossible to continue. For many years it was thought that Tello hid the city of Lagash, until an American expedition, working at the nearby site of al-Hiba, discovered evidence that al-Hiba was Lagash and Tello was Girsu.

De Sarzec and his workers excavated thousands of cuneiform tablets, but the local inhabitants were not idle between the French campaigns, and they retrieved almost forty thousand clay documents from Tello and sold them to antiquities dealers.

During the latter part of the reign of Naram-Sin, and through the early years of his successor Shar-kali-sharri, the governor of Lagash was named Lugal-ushumgal. By chance of discovery we know that he was a literate man, because he signed a beautifully inscribed six-sided clay prism inscribed with a copy of one of the most important scholarly word lists of the third millennium (Schileico 1914–15; Lambert 1979: 17-18). The end of the text reads: "Lugal-ushumgal, scribe, governor of Lagash."

Border Problems

4. RTC 83
(Sumerian)

1. [. . .]
2. [ù-na-dug$_4$]
3. ⌜puzur$_4$⌝-^{d}[ma-ma]
4. [én]si la[gaš^{ki}-ke$_4$]
5. na-bé-a
6. 1 su$_{11}$-lum^{ki}
7. 1 é-^{giš}apin^{ki}
8. ⌜u$_4$⌝ šar-ru-GI-t[a]
9. ki-sur-ra lagaš^{ki}-[kam]
10. ur-^{d}utu-ke$_4$
11. [n]am-énsi ⌜uri$_5$^{ki}⌝-ma
12. ⌜^{d}⌝na-ra-am-[^{d}en.zu-(ra)]
13. ⌜ì-na-ak⌝-ka
14. 2 ma-na kù-sig$_{17}$
15. kadra íb-ši-⌜ak⌝
16. ur-é énsi ⌜lagaš^{ki}-ke$_4$⌝
17. ⌜ba⌝-da-⌜kar⌝
18. ⌜è⌝-ni-[šè . . .]
19. [?] ⌜lagaš⌝[^{ki} . . .]
20. [. . .]
21. [. . .]
22. ḫé-éb-MI/GI[G]-[x]

[Tell so-and-so]: Thus says Puzur-Mama, governor of Lagash: Since the time of (King) Sargon (the hamlets of) Sulum and E-apin were on the border, within (the territory of) Lagash. Ur-Utu, who was governor of Ur under (King) Naram-Sin, made the gift of two minas of gold. (Now) Ure, governor of Lagash, has seized (the two hamlets). After he left [. . .] Lagash [. . .]. He should [. . .].

Personnel

5. ITT 1 1100
(Sumerian)

1. 1 gú-tar-lá
2. dumu sag-a-DU
3. DINGIR-mu-da
4. an-da-ti
5. du$_6$-lugal-u$_5$-a⌜^{ki}⌝-a
6. ab-tuš
7. 1 lugal-nam-dag
8. dumu ur-temen
9. inim-ma
10. nu-bànda
11. an-da-ti
12. bára-si-ga^{ki}-a ab-tuš
13. dumu nibru^{ki}-me
14. lagaš^{ki}-a
15. ab-durun$_x$(TUŠ.TUŠ)-né-éš
16. ḫa-mu-ra-ne-šúm-mu

Gutarla, the son of Sagadu, is living with Ili-muda. He dwells in Dulugalua. Lugal-namdag, the son of Ur-temen, is living with Inima, the sergeant. He dwells in (the hamlet of) Barasiga. They are citizens of Nippur; they are dwelling in (the territory of) Lagash. They are to be handed over to you.

6. ITT 1 1261
(Sumerian)

1. lugal-mu
2. en-níg-lu$_5$-lá-ke$_4$
3. na-bé-[a]
4. 4 dug kaš g[i$_6$]
5. 20 ninda gúg x [. . .]

X lines broken

1′. [. . .] x x [. . .]
2′. ⌜é⌝-gal-⌜šè⌝
3′. ⌜šu⌝ im-mi-ús$^?$ [. . . $^?$]
4′. lugal-mu
5′. géštu-ga-ni
6′. ḫé-zu

(Speak to) my lord: Thus says Enniglula: Four jugs of black beer (and) 20 breads . . . *dispatched* to the palace. May my lord lend an ear!

7. ITT 2/1 4523
(Sumerian)

1. ur-gidri
2. na-bé-⸢a⸣
3. ur-^{d}nin-ma[r^{ki}]
4. ù-na-dug$_4$
5. é lú-^{d}[x]
6. lú na-ni-[ib]-ku$_4$-k[u$_4$]
7. lú-[. . .]
8. šu ḫ̮é-[ba-re$_6$]
9. u$_4$ [. . .]
10. ki x [. . .]
11. si x [. . .]

Thus says Ur-gidri: Tell Ur-Ninmar that no one should enter the estate of Lu- . . . (and) that he is to release Lu-[x]. When . . .

8. ITT 1 1471
(Akkadian)

1. 1 lugal-èn-⸢tar⸣-sù MUHALDIM
2. ÁRAD qì-šum
3. *ìš-te$_4$*
4. lugal-ušumgal
5. ÉNSI
6. lagaš^{ki}
7. *u-ša-ab*
8. *li-ru-ù-nim*

(Tell) them to bring me the cook Lugal-entarsu, the servant/slave of (the general?) Qishum, who is living with Lugal-ushumgal, the governor of Lagash.

9. ITT 1 1080
(Akkadian)

1. [x] + 26 ŠE GUR
2. [ŠE.B]A 2 ITI.TA
3. MU 3.KAM
4. 8.0.0.0 LÁ 8.0.0 ŠE GUR
5. ŠE.BA 4 ITI.TA
6. [x] + 340 ^{túg}BAL
7. [. . .]

1′. [. . .]
2′. [X.BA] MU.4$^{?}$.KAM
3′. *šu* 285 ŠABRA
4′. lagaš^{ki}
5′. *en-ma*
6′. šar-ru-DÙG
7′. *a-na* lugal-ušumgal
8′. *[ar]-ḫ̮i-ìš*
9′. *[šu]-bí-lam*

7,800 (+) liters of grain—grain rations for two months—for three years; 141,600 liters of grain—grain rations for four months—340 BAL garments

[. . . x]—rations for *four* years—pertaining to 285 overseers. Tell Sharru-ṭab: Send (them) immediately to Lugal-ushumgal!

10. ITT 1 1103
(Akkadian)

1′. ÁRAD *ti-ab*
2′. *in* lagaš^{ki}
3′. *u-ša-bu*
1. *li-ru-nim*
2. *en-ma*
3. be-lí-BÀD
4. ⸢NU.BÀNDA⸣ LÚ.LUNGA
5. [. . .]

rest broken

[Tell so-and-so that he should] send [so-and-so], the servant of Ti'ab, who lives in Lagash, to me. Thus (says) Beli-duri: The overseer of the brewers. . . .

11. ITT 1 1265
(Akkadian)

1. šul-gig
2. šeš-kur-ra
3. a-zi
4. NU.BÀNDA
5. ur-nìgin
6. *[in]* lagaš$^{⸢ki⸣}$
7. *[u-ša]-bu*
8. *li-su-rí-am*

(Tell) him to send me Shulgig, Shesh-kura, Azi, the sergeant, (and) Ur-nigin, who are living in Lagash.

12. RTC 78
(Akkadian)

1. *en-ma*
2. sa-aṭ-pi-DINGIR
3. *a-na* É.GUD
4. *ši* GAL_5.LÁ
5. 1 lú-ba
6. DUMU lugal-ka
7. [1 sa]g-íl
8. [Á]RAD-*sú*
9. *li-tá-ar-kà-am-ma*
10. *iš̃-*te_4
11. lugal-ušumgal
12. *li-su-ṣi-áš̃-su-ni*

Thus (says) Shaṭpi-ilum to É.GUD, who works for the police: Luba, the son of Lugalka, (and) Sagil, his servant, should be . . . (and so) he should obtain the release of these two from Lugal-ushumgal.

Legal Affairs

13. ITT 2/2 5758
(Sumerian)

1. lugal-kù-zu
2. na-bé-a
3. lugal-ušumgal
4. ù-na-dug$_4$
5. [. . .]

X number of lines broken.

1′. [. . .]
2′. mu-ku$_5$
3′. ur-^{d}nin-gír-su
4′. ù nam-érim
5′. nu-ga-ma-ku$_5$
6′. di-bi di ḫé-bé

Thus says Lugal-kuzu: Tell Lugal-ushumgal . . . Ur-Ningirsu . . . and moreover he did not take the oath for me. (Tell him) that this matter should be brought to judgment.

14. STTI 73
(Sumerian)

1. eden-ba
2. na-bé-a
3. lugal-mu
4. ù-na-dug$_4$
5. ^{d}nisaba-an-dùl
6. má éren-a
7. [ki]-la[gaš$^{ki?}$ . . .]

1′. [. . .]
2′. éren-e ba-[x-x]-a[k-x$^{?}$]

Thus says Edenba: Tell His Majesty that Nisaba-andul [. . .] the ship with conscripts . . . the Lagash district. [. . .] the conscripts [. . .]

15. DPA 48
(Girsu?, Akkadian)

1. *en-ma*
2. da-da
3. *a-na* lugal-ra
4. ur-tur
5. *šu* amar-si$_4$
6. ŠE *a u-sá-dì-in*

Thus (says) Dada to Lugalra: He must not allow Ur-tur to collect the grain from Amarsi!

16. DPA 49
(Girsu?, Akkadian)

1. *en-ma*
2. da-da
3. *a-na* lugal-ra
4. 1 (SILÀ) BAPPIR SIG$_5$
5. 1 (SILÀ) MUNU$_4$ SIG$_5$
6. 3 (SILÀ) NÍG.ÀR.RA SIG$_5$
7. *a-na* šu-ì-lí-su
8. *li-dì-in*

Thus (says) Dada to Lugalra: He is to give Shu-ilishu one liter of good quality beer-cake, one liter of good quality malt, (and) three liters of good quality groats!

Real Estate Matters

17. STTI 11
(Sumerian)

1. 5 (bùr) GÁNA
2. [u]r-nu sanga
3. ⸢kúrum-bi⸣ ì-ak
4. ⸢x⸣-dun-a
5. ⸢ur⸣-gidri-ke$_4$
6. ⸢na⸣-bé-⸢a⸣
7. ⸢lugal-ka⸣
8. ḫé-me-šúm-m[u]
9. du$_6$-bu-ra^{ki}-ka
10. ì-gál

Urnu, the chief temple administrator, has inspected the five bur field. Thus say X-duna and Ur-gidri: (Tell) Lugalka to hand it over to us. It is located in (the hamlet of) Dubura.

18. ITT 5 6752
(Sumerian)

1. ur-^{d}ištar[an]
2. na-bé-a
3. lugal-mu
4. ù-na-dug$_4$
5. ⸢1⸣ é
6. ⸢ur⸣-gar lú kas$_4$-kam
7. 1 é
8. [. . . -kam]
9. 1 é
10. lugal-ezen-ke$_4$-kam
11. lugal-mu
12. ù-na-dug$_4$
13. bàd-e ⸢im⸣-ma-ná
14. D[A . . .]

Thus says Ur-Ishtaran: Tell His Majesty that one estate belongs to Ur-gar, the messenger, one estate belongs to [. . .], (and) one estate belongs to Lugalezen. Tell His Majesty: *They lay by the wall . . .*

19. ITT 1 1058
(Sumerian)

1. ⌜1⌝ a-na-ku-⌜zi⌝
2. gudu$_4$ ^{d}giš-bar-è
3. 1 é-ki nu-bànda gú-eden-na
4. nimgir-èš
5. na-bé-a
6. lugal-ušumgal
7. ù-na-dug$_4$
8. ú-tá
9. ḫa-mu-na-šúm-mu

(Concerning) Anakuzi, the priest of (the god) Gishbare (and) Eki, the inspector of the Guedena (borderland). Thus says Nimgiresh: Tell Lugalushumgal to give (them) to Uta.

20. ITT 1 1170
(Sumerian)

1. lú-ba nu-bànda
2. na-bé-a
3. lugal-mu
4. ù-na-dug$_4$
5. lú-zàḫ
6. dumu a-zu-zu
7. éren-a ì-gub
8. da-da
9. dumu nigar
10. é-ni ba-du$_7$
11. šu ḫé-ba-re$_6$

Thus says Luba, the sergeant: Tell His Majesty (or: Lugalmu) that Luzah (or: the runaway), the son of Azuzu, is serving in the army. Dada, the son of Nigar, has *seized* his estate, but he is to release it.

Sargonic Letters from Adab

Adab, modern Bismaya, was excavated at the beginning of this century by E. J. Banks on behalf of the University of Chicago. The expedition uncovered more than nine hundred Old Akkadian tablets from two different parts of the site, from a room in what was probably an official building, and from a set of private houses. Two thirds of these tablets await study in Istanbul; the texts that were deposited in the Oriental Institute in Chicago have been analyzed in a recent work by Yang (1989).

The major portion of the administrative texts from Adab date from the time of Shar-kali-sharri (2217–2193 BCE), the last major ruler of the Akkad dynasty.

Affairs of Ishkun-Dagan

These two letters, written in a beautiful Old Akkadian hand, were not officially excavated at Adab, but on internal evidence one assumes that they originated there. The Ishkun-Dagan who wrote these letters must have been an important man in the city, and it may be that he was the same person as the owner of an exquisite seal, also of unknown origin, inscribed with the words: "O Shar-kali-sharri, king of the subjects of (the god) Enlil and O Queen Tuta-shar-libbish—Ishkun-Dagan, scribe, the majordomo, is your servant!" (Buchannan 1981: 445). Although there can be no certainty that both of these letters were addressed by the same person, they share a highly rhetorical style.

21. Thureau-Dangin, *RA* 23:25
(Adab?, Akkadian)

1. *en-ma*
2. iš-ku-un-^{d}da-gan
3. *a-na* puzur$_4$-^{d}eštar
4. ^{d}INANNA
5. *ù* ìl-a-ba$_4$
6. ^{d}ašgi (AŠ.ŠIR.GI$_4$)
7. *ù* ^{d}nin-ḫur-sag
8. *na-ʾà-âš* LUGAL
9. *ù na-ʾà-âš* NIN
10. *lu tu-mu-at*
11. *a-dî e-né-a*
12. *la tá-mu-ru*
13. NINDA ⸢KAŠ⸣ *la ta-la-ʿà-mu*
14. *ù [a]-dî la tág-ru-⸢sa⸣-am*
15. *in* ^{giš}GU.ZA
16. *la tu-sa-bu*

Thus (says) Ishkun-Dagan to Puzur-Eshtar: You must take the oath by Inanna and Ilaba (the gods of Agade), by Ashgi and Ninhursaga (the gods of Adab), (and) by the life of the king and the life of the queen, that until you meet me, you will take neither food nor drink (lit., bread nor beer), and that until you have *come* to me, you will not (even) sit down in a chair!

22. Smith, *JRAS* 1932:296
(Adab?, Akkadian)

1. *en-ma*
2. iš-ku-un-^{d}da-gan
3. *a-na* LUGAL.RA
4. AŠA$_5$-*lam ʾà-ru-uš*
5. *ù* MÁŠ.ANŠE *ù-ṣú-ur*
6. *a-pu-na-ma*
7. *gu-ti-um-ma-mì*
8. AŠA$_5$-*lam*

9. *ù-la a-ru-uš*
10. *a taq-bí*
11. *a-na* 1/2 ⸢DA⸣.NA.TA
12. *ma-ag-ga-ti*
13. *su-si-ib-ma*
14. *at-tá*
15. AŠA$_5$-*lam* *'à-ru-uš*
16. *ki* GURUŠ.GURUŠ
17. *ú-wa-kà-mu*
18. *ti-bu-tám*
19. *li-se*$_{11}$*-ù-ni-kum-ma*
20. MÁŠ.ANŠE *a-na* URU^{ki}-*lim*
21. *su-tá-rí-ib*
22. ⸢*šum*⸣-*ma* MÁŠ.ANŠE-*mì*
23. *gu*-⸢*ti*⸣-*ù it*-⸢*ru*⸣-*ù*
24. *ù a-na-ku*$_8$
25. *mí-ma ù-la a-qá-bi*
26. ⸢KÙ.BABBAR⸣-*am a-na-da-kum*
27. ⸢*a*⸣-*ni*
28. *na-'à-aš* šar-kà-lí-šàr-rí
29. *ù-má*
30. *šum-ma* MÁŠ.ANŠE
31. *gu-ti-ù it-ru-ù*
32. *in ra-ma-ni-kà*
33. *lu tá-na-da-nu*
34. *a-na-lim-ma ki a-la-kam*
35. KÙ.BABBAR-*am a-na-da-nu-kum*
36. *ù at-tá* MÁŠ.ANŠE
37. *ù-la tá-na-ṣa-ar*
38. *iš-pí-kí*
39. *gi-nu-tim*
40. *a-rí-iš-kà*
41. MU.DUG *lu ti-da*

Thus (says) Ishkun-Dagan to Lugalra: Work the field and guard the flocks! Just don't say to me: "It is (the fault of) the Gutians; I could not work the land!" Man *outposts* every mile, and then you will be able to work the land! If the soldiers attack, you can raise help and have the herd brought into the city. In the event that (you tell me) "the Gutians have rustled the flocks," I will say nothing about it and (just) pay you the money. Look here, I swear by the life of (King) Shar-kali-sharri that if the Gutians rustle the flocks, and you have to pay from your own assets, I will (re)pay you the money when I arrive in town. But even if you don't succeed in guarding the herds, I will ask you for the correct (amount) of the field rent (that you owe me)! . . . you should know (this)!

The Affairs of Mr. Mezi

The next four letters (nos. 23-26) were written from, and to, a certain Mezi. The name is absent from all the known texts from Adab, and therefore one cannot establish his identity, if indeed only one person is involved. The letters are written in either Sumerian or Akkadian, and one letter appears to mix the two, with the salutation in Akkadian and the body of the missive in Sumerian. The phrase "to my lord" is rendered here as "to His Majesty," on the assumption that the letters were addressed to the king, most likely to Shar-kali-sharri. One deduces that Mezi was a high-ranking official, an important businessman, or both. There was clearly someone above him, as the letter from Angu indicates. There was a general named Angu at

Adab (Yang 1989: 373), but there is no assurance that this was the same person as the author of that letter.

23. Yang, Adab A 868
(Sumerian)

1. ⸢me-zi⸣
2. na-bé-a
3. lugal-níg-zu
4. ù-na-dug$_4$
5. 1 ama-làl
6. géme é-aš[gab]
7. ⸢árad-gá⸣
8. du$_6$^{ki}-šè ba-zàḫ
9. ḫa-mu-ra-šúm-mu

Thus says Mezi: Amalal, a servant girl from the leatherworker's establishment, (who) is my slave has escaped to (the hamlet of) Du. (Tell) Lugal-nigzu to give her to you.

24. Yang, Adab A 706
(Akkadian)

1. *en-[ma]*
2. me-z[i]
3. *a-na be-lí*
4. 10 GIŠ.KIN.TI
5. ⸢3⸣ ÀZLAG
6. *tup-pí-su-ni*
7. LÚ.KIN.GI$_4$.A ⸢LUGAL⸣
8. *u-ub-lam*
9. *[n]a-'à-áš-su ù-má*
10. *[2?] su$_4$-ni-ti*
11. [x?] KIN LUGAL
12. [. . . L]UGAL
13. [L]Ú? URU^{ki}-*lim*
14. [. . .] *ba* [. . .]
15. [. . . *i]n* ada[b^{ki}]
16. *la u-áš-b[u]*
17. *be-lí*
18. *'à-wa-a-ti*
19. ⸢*li*⸣-*[iš?]*-⸢*me?*⸣
20. *in* [. . .]
21. *li-i[k . . .]*
22. *'à-si$_4$-at*
23. *be-*⸢*lam*⸣ *la* [. . .]

Thus (says) Mezi to His Majesty: Concerning the ten craftsmen and three fullers; the king's envoy has brought the inscribed tablets of the two (groups of personnel) to me. I swear by his life: the two of them . . . king . . . in the city . . . They are not living in Adab. May His Majesty listen to my report! He should . . . The Lord . . . not . . .

25. Yang, Adab A 830
(Sumerian/Akkadian)

1. *a-na be-l[í]*
2. *en-m[a]*
3. *me-z[i]*
4. 2 (bur'u) GÁNA im-m[a]
5. lugal-m[u]
6. in-na-[šúm$^{?}$]
7. la-ba-gi-in
8. [ig]i$^{?}$ bí-in-ra-š[è]
9. [m]u$^{?}$-su-ga-b[i-šè]

Rest of obverse broken

1′. dumu x
2′. [lu]gal-mu ⌜ab⌝-[. . .]
3′. [. . .]
4′. še-bi 240 [. . .]
5′. ga-an-[su$^{?}$ . . .]

Thus (says) Mezi to His Majesty: The 360 iku field which my lord gave to him last year has not been confirmed. . . . *because of its return* . . . son . . . my lord . . . I want to return its grain . . .

26. Yang, Adab A 942
(Sumerian)

1. an-gú-e
2. na-bé-a
3. me-zi-ra
4. ù-na-dug$_4$
5. má-gur$_8$-šè
6. ḫé-ši-kalag
7. en-ne-ne
8. ù bar-ra-an
9. ḫa-mu-ne-gi$_4$-gi$_4$

Thus says Angu: Tell Mezi that he is to repair the boats and return them to Enene and Bara'an.

Mr. Ungal's Donkey and Other Matters

27. Yang, Adab A 661
(Sumerian)

1. [PN-(ra)]
2. [ù-na]-dug$_4$
3. nam-tar-ré-e
4. na-bé-a
5. 1 anše
6. un-gal-ka
7. šu-ni-DINGIR dub-sar
8. ba-an-de$_6$
9. 1 ì-sa$_6$-s[a$_6$]
10. [. . .]

11. [. . .]
12. é ur-^{giš}gígir
13. dumu lugal-ka-ke_4
14. ba-ab-$la\breve{h}_4$-$\breve{h}$e-éš
15. 1 (bùr) GÁNA ki-giš-ì-ka
16. šabra é-ke_4
17. [$\breve{h}$a-mu-n]a-šúm-ma-a
18. [. . .]-⌜uru_4⌝?
19. [. . .]

Tell [so-and-so]: Thus says Namtare: Shuni-DINGIR, the scribe, has taken away a donkey belonging to Ungal (or: the general). Isasa [and . . .] have been taken to the estate of Ur-gigir, the son of Lugalka. One bur of land in the sesame (field), which the majordomo had given him [. . .]

The Death of a Messenger

This laconic letter was written by Lugal-gish, the governor of Adab during the reign of Shar-kali-sharri. The recipient, Lugal-mashkim, is not otherwise attested. The letter was found on "Mound IV" of Adab, in the same room as all the other Old Akkadian administrative texts. We know nothing of the precise provenance of the other letters from the city.

28. Yang, Adab 4
(Sumerian)

1. [lu]gal-giš-e
2. na-bé-a
3. lugal-maškim-e
4. ⌜ù⌝-na-dug_4
5. [l]ú kin-g[i_4-a]-m[u]
6. [l]ú mu-ga[z]
7. [in]im?-b[i x $\breve{h}$]é-e[m- . . .]
8. [ki-babbar]-ra^{ki}-šè
9. $\breve{h}$é-eb-bal-e

Thus says Lugal-gish: Tell Lugal-mashkim that (since) my messenger has been killed, he is to [. . .] the matter, and to relay it to (the town of) Kibabar.

A Petition to the King

The following fragmentary letter, addressed by an otherwise unknown individual to king Shar-kali-sharri, is unique among early Mesopotamian epistles. The elaborate invocation reminds one of later literary letters of petition.

29. Yang, Adab A 874
(Sumerian)

1. [i]gi-bar-e
2. ⌜na⌝-bé-a
3. érin kalam-ma
4. ki-ág dingir-maḫ
5. ki-ág ^{d}ašgi (AŠ.ŠIR.GI$_4$)
6. [x šá]r-kà-lí-[ša]r-rí-ra
7. [. . .]
8. [. . .]
9. [x an]še [. . .]-x-ka
   [. . .]-šúm
10. ⌜ki-duru$_5$ nu⌝-tuku
11. ⌜ki⌝-duru$_5$ ⌜na-me ḫa⌝-
    [m]a-ab-šúm-mu

Thus says Igibar: [Speak] to the *yoke* of the land, to the beloved of (the goddess) Dingir-mah, the beloved of (the god) Ashgi (. . .) to (King) Shar-kali-sharri . . .   . . . donkey . . . gave. I have no watered land parcel; (tell him) to give me whatever watered parcel is available.

Ilish-takal Wants a Chariot

30. Yang, Adab A 636
(Sumerian)

1. lugal-mu
2. ù-na-dug$_4$
3. ì-lí-iš-ta-kál-e na-bé-a
4. [1] ⌜^{giš}⌝gígir é-UMBIN × UDU-2
5. [b]a-ma in-na-dug$_4$
6. ⌜nu⌝-ma-ba
7. è-ni-šè
8. ki-babbar-ra^{ki}-ka
9. é ba-zi-zi-ka
10. 1 ^{giš}gígir é-UMBIN × UDU-2
11. al-gál
12. lú-mu igi im-mi-du$_8$-àm
13. lú kin-gi$_4$-a-ka-ni
14. ù-mu-gi$_4$
15. ḫa-ma-ab-šúm-mu
16. árad kalag-ga-ni-me-en$_6$
17. ga-na šà-mu ḫé-eb-ḫúl-le
18. im-sar-ra-⌜bi⌝
19. [ig]i-ni-šè ⌜ḫé$^{?}$-gál⌝
20. ur$_5$-e ⌜géštug⌝-ga-na
21. ḫé-na-[ni]-⌜íb-tuk-tuk⌝
22. ù gá-e šà-ga-ni
23. ab-ḫúl-le-en$_6$

Tell my lord: Thus says Ilish-takal: I told him: "give me the two-wheeled chariot!" But he did not give it to me. While he was away, my man had seen that there was a two-wheeled chariot in Kibabar, in the house of Bazizi. Then, after his messenger is dispatched, he should give (the chariot) to me.

Come on, I am his stalwart servant, surely he can make me happy! Therefore put this inscribed tablet before him, so that he may hear how it is, and I will also make him happy.

Various Economic Matters

31. Yang, Adab A 748 (Akkadian)

1. *a-na* ÉNSI
2. *en-ma*
3. wu-túr-be-lí
4. 20 ŠE GUR a-ga-dè^{ki}
5. *ĩš-te*$_4$
6. en-an-na-túm
7. *àm-ḫur*

Thus (says) Wutur-beli to the city governor: I have received 9,000 liters of barley by the Agade measure from Eanatum.

32. Yang, Adab A 963 (Sumerian)

1. [e]n-abzu-x[. . .]
2. na-bé-[a]
3. ur-é-maḫ luga[l-mu]
4. ù-na-dug$_4$
5. 1 [m]a-na síg
6. [. . .] x [. . .]
7. [. . .]
8. [. . .]
9. [. . .]
10. [. . .] ⸢dam-ke$_4$⸣
11. [na-b]é-a
12. ⸢ur⸣-é-maḫ šeš-[mu]
13. ù-na-[dug$_4$]
14. ⸢é$^?$⸣-gá bar IG[I . . .]
15. [an]še$^?$ ša x [. . .]
16. [x]x-bi šu ḫa-[ma]-⸢ús⸣

Thus says Enabzu: Tell Ur-Emah, my lord, that one mina of wool [. . .]. Thus says [so and so]: Speak to Ur-Emah, [*my*] brother: . . . my courtyard . . . he should dispatch its . . . to me.

33. Yang, Adab A 695 (Sumerian)

1. 9 ni-is-ku
2. 27 šà-dug$_4$
3. ugula ^{d}en-líl-lá
4. 1 má šà-da

5. [x] má x ^{d}x
X *lines broken*
1′. [. . .]
2′. [na]-bé-a
3′. [l]ugal-mu
4′. ù-na-dug$_4$
5′. ḫa-mu-ra-ab-šúm-mu

Nine persons of the nisku class (and) 27 infants; the overseer is Enlila. One shada boat [so many x type] boats [. . .]. Thus says [so-and-so]: Tell my lord to give them to you.

Sargonic Letters from Gasur

Gasur is the earliest known name of the settlement later known as Nuzi, located at the modern site of Yorghan Tepe, to the east of the modern city of Kirkuk. Most of the 222 Sargonic tablets that were excavated there by an American expedition between 1928 and 1931 probably come from one large archive (Meek 1935: viii). The majority of the texts concern the administration of state lands, although other matters are also addressed. It has been suggested that this is the archive of a household that was directly under the control of the central government (Foster 1982d: 48).

The Distribution of Grain Rations

34. HSS 10 5
(Akkadian)

1. *en-ma* da-da
2. *a-na* ì-lí
3. *qí-bí-ma*
4. ŠE *šu a-na* ŠE.BA
5. *a-si-tu*
6. *a-na* ŠE.NUMUN
7. *li-sa-mì-id-ma*
8. *li-dì-in*
9. *ù šum-ma*
10. *si-mu-ur$_4$-rí-ù*^{ki}
11. *a-dì da-ni-iš*
12. ŠE *la i-ma-ḫa-ru*
13. *in qir-bí-su*
14. *a-na* ŠE.BA *li-dì-in*
15. *a-na-ku$_8$ a-kà-sa-ar*
16. *ù pá-ni* ENGAR.ENGAR
17. *li-ṣú-ur-ma*
18. *e-re-su-nu*
19. *li-ṣú-ru da-ni-iš*
20. *ù a-na* 1 pu-zu-zu
21. DUMU zu-zu ŠE.BA *a i-dì-in*
22. *a-na ni-qí-im* SÁ *šum-ma*
23. *e-ra-si-iš na-ṭú*
24. [ŠE.NU]MUN *li-zi-ib*
25. *su$_4$-be-la*

Thus (says) Dada, say to Ili: He should assign the grain that I had left over for rations as seed grain and give it out. But in case the Simureans do not receive enough grain (to eat), he should give out some of it as grain rations;

I will replace it myself. Moreover, he should take care of the farmers and diligently safeguard their plots, but he should not give any grain rations to Puzuzu, son of Zuzu, (as) it is *reserved for the offering.* If it is suitable for planting, he should leave seed grain behind.

Notation: Shu-bela.

35. HSS 10 6
(Akkadian)

1. *[e]n-ma* da-da
2. *[a-n]a* su$_{4}$-ma-DINGIR
3. DABIN *šu iš-te$_{4}$-su*
4. *li-ṣú-ur*
5. LUGAL-*um*
6. *è-la-kam*
7. *ù a-na* ì-lí
8. *qí-bí-ma*
9. [. . .]x ŠE$^{?}$ [. . .]x

Rest of obverse broken

Reverse

1′. [. . .]
2′. [. . .] NI [. . .]
3′. [. . .] *i*-T[I . . .]

Approximately 8 lines broken

1″. *[l]i-se$_{11}$-rí-am*
2″. [T]ÚG$^{?}$ ù ⌜Ì.GIŠ$^{?}$⌝
(*perhaps to be inserted above*)

Thus (says) Dada to Shuma-ilum: He should take care of the grain-meal which is in his care! The king is coming here! Moreover, say to Ili: . . . grain . . . he gave . . . he should send me *garments and oil.*

36. HSS 10 7
(Akkadian)

1. *[e]n-ma*
2. da-da
3. *a-na* ì-lí
4. *qí-bí-ma*
5. ṣa-lí-lí
6. *li-li-am*

Thus (says) Dada, speak to Ili: Ṣalili is to come here to me!

37. HSS 10 10
(Akkadian)

1. *en-m[a]*
2. ur-sa$_{6}$
3. *a-na* ì-lí
4. *qí-bí-ma*

5. [1] a-ḫu-su_4-nu
6. 1 ne-sa-sa
7. 1 ì-lí-iš-tá-kál
8. *in* É *ki-šè-er-tim*
9. *[a-d]ì-ma*
10. *[a]-la-kam*
11. *li-ĩš-bu*
12. 1 GÚN GÚ GAL.GAL
13. 1 GÚN GÚ TUR.TUR
14. *li-se_{11}-bi-lam*

Thus (says) Ursa, Speak to Ili: Ahushunu, Nesasa, (and) Ilish-takal are to remain in prison until I arrive. (Moreover), he should send me one talent of broad beans, and one talent of peas.

38. HSS 10 11
(Akkadian)

1. *[en-ma]*
2. [PN]
3. *[a-na]* ⸢ì-lí⸣
4. *[qí-b]í-ma*
5. [ŠE.NU]MUN $GARAŠ_4^{sar}$
6. *[l]i-se_{11}-bi-lam*
7. *ù šum-ma*
8. ì-lí-be-lí
9. *ù* iš-má-DINGIR
10. *la-ba-a*
11. *[er-r]e-[s]u-nu*
12. *[l]i-iṣ-ba-at*

Rest of tablet broken.

[Thus (says) so-and-so], Speak to Ili: He should send me leek seeds. Moreover, should Ili-beli and Ishma'-ilum . . . , he should seize their tenant plot.

39. HSS 10 12
(Akkadian)

1. *[en-ma]*
2. [PN]
3. *[a-na PN]*
4. *[qí-bí-ma]*

Undetermined number of lines missing.

1′. *ba-[lu?]-um*
2′. ÉNSI
3′. *a-na* kí-nu-ús-sa-am
4′. *ù* $puzur_4$-^{d}sìn
5′. *a e-ru-ub*
6′. *a-dì* ÉNSI
7′. ⸢*la ù-we-e-ru-uš*⸣

Rest broken

[Thus (says) so-and-so, Speak to so-and-so]: . . . should not enter into service of Kinushsham and Puzur-Sin without the (*permission*) of the city governor. Until I have not sent him to the governor . . .

Sargonic Letters from Kish

Kish was undoubtedly the most important northern Babylonian political center prior to the ascent of the Akkad dynasty. With the rise of neighboring Akkad, Kish lost much of its importance, but it remained an important economic center at least into the sixteenth century BCE.

40. MAD 5 2
(Akkadian)

1. *en-ma*
2. ab-ba-a-a
3. *a-na* du-du-a
4. *mi-núm*
5. *ù-la a-bí at-tá*
6. *ma a-na* 10 ŠE GUR
7. *ù-la tá-qí-pá-an-ni*
8. É *e-rí*
9. *šum-ma* KÙ.BABBAR
10. *è-rí-šu-kà*
11. *[a-n]a*? 20 GUR
12. [1/3] ŠA GÍN ⌜*lu-sa*⌝-*bí-l[a]-kum*
13. *šum-ma* ⌜*a*⌝-*na* SAG
14. *[m]a*? *lu-sa-[bí-la]-kum*
15. *[a]t-tá šu-ṣí-a-am*
16. ⌜*ù*⌝ DUMU-*kà* ⌜*šu*⌝-*up*-⌜*ra-šum*⌝-*ma*
17. *[su*$_4$*-m]a*? *li-iš-me*

Thus (says) Abbaja to Dudu'a: What (is the matter)? You are not (acting as if you were) my father! What—you don't (even) trust me with 3,000 liters of grain? The house is empty! Should someone request silver from you, I will send you (silver) for 6,000 liters of grain, at (the rate of) a third of a shekel (per 300 liters). O you—release (the grain) to me and send your son here so that he may hear (about it) *himself!*

41. MAD 5 22
(Akkadian)

1. 1 *a-dì*-DINGIR
2. *iš-te*$_4$
3. 1 DINGIR-dan
4. *ši* šu-ì-lí-su
5. SAG.DU$_5$
6. ÁRAD DINGIR-ba-ni
7. DAM.GÀR
8. ÁRAD šar-a-ti-gu-bi-si-in
9. *u-ša-ab*
10. *li-ru-nim*
11. dingir-gú
12. MAŠKIM

Adi-Ilum is living with Ilum-dan *of the clan* of Shu-ilishu, the field registrar, (who is) in the service of Ilum-bani the merchant, (who is) in the service of Shar-addi-gubishin. Bring him to me. Dingir-gu is (to be) the conveyor.

42. MAD 5 54
(Akkadian)

1. *en-ma*
2. ÁRAD-sú-ni
3. *a-na* tá-áš-má-tum
4. 1 èr-e-bum
5. *ù* 1 bí-la-LUM
6. LÚ.ZÀḪ.ME
7. *su-ma*
8. *e-la-kà-tiš*$_{11}$
9. *ṣa-ab-t[i]-su-⌜ni?-ti⌝*

Thus (says) Warassuni to Tashmatum: Errebum and Bilalum are fugitives. If they come *here,* seize them both!

Old Akkadian Letters from Eshnunna

43. MAD 1 185
(Akkadian)

1. *en-ma*
2. be-lí-ba-ni
3. *a-na* ì-za-za
4. *su-lum-ki*
5. *su-bí-lim*
6. *ù* a-la-la
7. *sal*$_{4}$*-ma-at*
8. *a-ḫa-tá-ki*
9. *sá-lim-tá*
10. 1 ⌜túg⌝BAL
11. *su-bí-lim*

Thus (says) Beli-bani to Izaza: How is your health? (lit., send me (news) of your health). On other matters: Alala is well and your two sisters are well. Send me a BAL garment!

44. MAD 1 282
(Eshnunna?, Akkadian)

1. *en-ma*
2. šu-ma-ma
3. *a-na* É.GI$_{4}$.A
4. 4 GÍN 1 MA.NA TUR KÙ.BABBAR
5. ìr-e-um
6. *íl-qè-ma*
7. *a-na* kà-bar-tim
8. *i-dì-in*

9. *šum-ma-sa*
10. *tá-na-kir*
11. [s]i-ir-kum
12. *[a-na]* AB+ÁŠ-*bu-tim*
13. *[li?]-šè-ib*

Thus (says) Shu-Mama to Kallatum: Ir'eum has taken four shekels and one smaller mina of silver and given it to Kabartum. Should she (Kabartum) deny (that this occurred), Shirkum should be present as a witness (to the transaction).

45. MAD 1 290
(Eshnunna?, Akkadian)

Obverse

1. *en-ma*
2. š[u]-ma-ma
3. *a-na* É.GI$_4$.A
4. *ù* eš$_4$-tár-ré-⌜ṣi⌝
5. *ù* DAM-X
6. *ù a-na* DUMU.NITA
7. *a-na* ri-ba-tum
8. *[ù] a-na kà-lí* É GÉME
9. *[qí-bí-ma]*
10. [. . . *-i]š*
11. [. . .]*-gu*

Rest of obverse broken

Reverse

1′. [. . .] ⌜*ù?*⌝ *a-na* eš$_{15}$-nun[ki]
2′. *[l]i-it-ru-ù-nim*
3′. *[ù] su-lum* É *kà-lí-su*
4′. *[i]n* DUB *li-iš-tu-ru-nim*
5′. 2 (PI) NÍG.ÀR.RA
6′. *ù e-tim-tá-su*
7′. *ni-se$_{11}$-bí-lam*
8′. 4 (PI) DABIN 2 (PI) ZÍD GU
9′. 2 SÌLA Ì DU$_{10}$.GA 2 SÌLA Ì
10′. *á-dum mi-nim*
11′. *la è-e-sa-ru-ni*
12′. ⌜*šu*⌝ 1 ÁRAD i-su-a
13′. [. . .] *la i-e-sa-ru*

Thus says Shu-Mama to Kallatum, and to Eshtar-reṣi, and to *his wife,* and to (his) son; to Ribatum [and] to the whole establishment of female servants, [Speak]: . . . .

. . . .And they should take [. . .] to Eshnunna and write down on a tablet (news) of the well-being of the whole household. We are now sending two liters of groats and its . . . . Why do they not . . . me concerning the 240 liters of barley-flour, 120 liters of pea flour, two liters of fine oil and two liters of ordinary oil? They did not . . . *a servant of Isua.*

46. MAD 1 298
(Eshnunna?, Akkadian)

1. *en-ma*
2. [u]-ṣi-um
3. ⌜*a*⌝*-na* šu-ma-ma
4. *ù* ⌜DINGIR⌝-dan

5. *ù šum-x-[s]u*
6. *a-ṣi-ḫa-mì*
7. *da-ni-ĩš da-ni-ĩš*
8. *ù en-m[a]*
9. [u-ṣi-um$^?$]
10. *[a-na]*
11. nu-ni-tum
12. eš$_4$-tár-tù-kúl-ti
13. *ù* il-la-at
14. MU (MUḪALDIM$^?$)
15. *a-ṣi-ḫ[a-mì]*
16. *da-ni-ĩš da-ni-ĩš*

Thus (says) Uṣ'ium to Shu-Mama and Ilum-dan and to Shum-x: I am extremely distressed! Furthermore, thus (says) [Uṣi'um to] Nunitum, Eshtar-tukulti, and Illat, *the cook:* I am extremely distressed!

47. OAIC 53
(Eshnunna?, Akkadian)

1. ⌜*en*⌝*-ma*
2. i-ku$_8$-núm
3. *[a-n]a* DINGIR-al-su
4. *[m]i-šum*
5. *[á]š-tu-ru*
6. ⌜*a*⌝*-ni-ìr-kum*
7. ⌜*si*⌝*-tum*
8. *ḫa-*⌜*ra-nam*⌝
9. *a-ḫu-z[a-a]m*
10. [. . .]
11. [. . . *-d]a-ba*
12. AŠA$_5$ *a-na* su$_4$-be-lí
13. *[i]-dì-in*
14. ZÍD.BA-*su*
15. *ù-la e-pi$_5$-ĩš*

Thus (says) Ikunum to Ilum-alshu: *Why do you think that* I wrote to you . . . ? I have taken to the road . . . He gave the/a field to Shu-beli. I will not prepare his flour ration.

Letters from Mugdan

Mugdan, modern Umm El-Jir, in the proximity of Kish, was a small town dominated by a large private household. Although none of the tablets from this site are from controlled excavations, there is good reason to believe that at least forty-two documents, in various museums, can be ascribed to the archive. Modern excavations carried out there in the late sixties failed to provide any new texts (Gibson 1972).

The Mugdan archive came from a large household, perhaps the dominant one in the town. It has been suggested that the unit controlled at least 2,756 acres of land (Foster 1982b: 37). It has also been suggested that the household was directly controlled by the royal family, but this is a matter open to debate (Foster 1982b: 37). Of the three letters from Mugdan, two are simple orders from one Zuzu, and the third is a short missive from a certain Shuma-ṣaba', concerning the administration of a parcel of specific land. A separate document from the same town lists numerous fields and their owners or lessees, including one by the same name, associated with Shuma-ṣaba', the "captain" (MAD 5 67: ii 6-8). It is described as having an area of twenty-four iku, that is, approximately 384 acres.

48. MAD 5 81
(Akkadian)

1. *en-ma*
2. zu-zu
3. *a-na* ša-aṭ-pum
4. 1.0.0 ŠE GUR
5. *a-na* šu-ì-lí-su
6. *li-dì-in*

Thus says Zuzu to Shaṭpum: Let him give 300 liters of barley to Shu-ilishu.

49. MAD 5 75
(Akkadian)

1. *[en]-ma*
2. [zu]-zu
3. *a-na* pù-su-su
4. ⌜*iš*⌝-*te*$_4$
5. [šu-ì]-lí-su
6. [x] + 3 GÍN ⌜ZABAR⌝
7. *li-il-qá*
8. *[a-na* x*]*
9. ⌜*li*⌝-*dì-in*

Thus says Zuzu to Pususu: Let him take three (+) shekels of bronze from Shu-ilishu and give it [to so-and-so].

50. MAD 5 83
(Akkadian)

1. *en-ma*
2. su$_4$-ma-ṣa-ba
3. *a-na* su-lí-um
4. *a e-ni-im*
5. AŠA$_5$
6. *ša* KÁ KIŠ BI-MU-UT
7. *ni-ti-qú*
8. *li-iš-qí-ù*

Thus says Shuma-ṣaba to Suli'um: Do not let it *get overgrown!* (Tell) him to water the . . . field of the Kish gate, *which we passed by (the last time).*

Letters from the "Mesag Archive"

The "Mesag" archive consists of 148 tablets that contain the records of an unidentified site in Sumer named Sagub, somewhere in the Umma-Lagash area (Bridges 1981; Steinkeller and Postgate 1992: 8-10). It is possible that the archive was actually housed in Umma. Most of the texts concern agricultural matters, and it seems likely that they derive from a large estate connected with state organization, most probably a royal estate. The head of the establishment, or of the office on the estate that was the source of the tablets, appears to have been one Mesag, who was probably also the governor of Umma, hence the conventional name for the archive. His official titles were: "city governor," "scribe," and "land registrar."

51. Fish, *MCS* 4:3 (Unknown, Akkadian)

1. *en-ma*
2. i-dì-èr-ra
3. *a-na* me-ság
4. 135 (GUR) 25 SÌLA ŠE GUR MAḪ
5. *[si]-tum*
6. *[iš]-te*$_4$*-su*
7. *ib*?*-si-su*
8. *ù* 420 ŠE GUR MAḪ
9. *šu* i-šar-⸢be⸣-lí
10. *i-dì-nu-šum*
11. ŠU.NÍGIN 555 (GUR) 25 SÌLA ŠE GUR MAḪ
12. [še]š-mu
13. *[si]-tum-ma*
14. [. . .]-mu
15. *iš-te*$_4$*-su*
16. *i-ba-šè*
17. *á-ni*
18. *ki-na-tu-ì-⸢a⸣*
19. *in bu-bu-tim*
20. *⸢i⸣-mu-tu*
21. *ki-ma* ŠE.BA
22. *[ku]-ti-ù*
23. *[m]a-ḫi-ru*
24. [L]UGAL
25. *i-da*
26. *ar-ḫi-iš*
27. *[li]-šè-er*
28. *⸢i⸣-dam*
29. *[be]-lí*
30. *[š]u-ku-un*
31. [3? +]3 MU 7 ITI

Thus (says) Iddin-Erra to Mesag: He had a remainder of 32,425 liters of grain, as well as 100,800 liters of grain which Ishar-beli had given him, (that is) a total of 133,225 liters of grain. Sheshmu has the rest . . . . *Look here,* my people are dying from hunger, while (even) the Gutians get rations! The king knows about it, so he (Mesag) better do something about it at once! Help me, my lord. Year 3 (+), month 7.

52. Donald, *MCS* 9:251
(Unknown, Akkadian)

1. *en-ma*
2. ⌜ŠABRA⌝ É
3. *a-na* me-ság
4. 11 DUG 10 (SÌLA) Ì ÁB
5. 20 DUG 20 (SÌLA) Ì NUN
6. 3.1.0 GA.ÀRA GUR
7. *a-na* da-da
8. [*ši*?] i-dì-èr-ra
9. [*a*?*-n*]*a*? UZ.GA
10. [*l*]*i-dì-in*
11. [e]n-ùri
12. DUB.SAR.E
13. MU.DE$_6$
14. [X] MU 7 ITI

Thus the estate manager to Mesag: He is to give 11 ten-liter jars of butter, 20 twenty-liter jars of ghee, 780 liters of cheese to Dada, [the subordinate?] of Iddin-Erra, for the uzga (temple). Enuri, the scribe, has delivered (the goods). Year [x], month 7.

53. ITT 4/1 7001 = MVN 6 1
(Sumerian)

1. me-ság-e
2. na-bé-a
3. mu-lugal
4. ur-lum-ma-ra
5. lú ba-ra-ba-dù
6. túg ba-ùr
7. 1 lugal-lú
8. ì-rá-rá
9. 1 da-da
10. dumu lugal-an-dùl
11. 1 da-da
12. àga-uš lugal
13. 1 bar-ra-an
14. 1 i-šar-a-ḫi
15. 1 nin-íd nar
16. 1 lú-^{d}nanše mu-sar
17. 1 DINGIR-mu-da
18. šu-nígin 8 lú ki-inim-ma-bi-me

Thus says Mesag: In the name of the king (I declare that) no one is to detain Ur-lumma! He has given up all claims (in the matter). Lugallu, the perfumer, Dada, son of Lugal-andul, Dada, royal guard, Bara'an, Ishar-ahi, Ninid, the cantor, Lu-Nanshe, *writing engraver,* (and) Ili-muda. In total eight witnesses thereof.

54. USP 63
(Sumerian)

1. 3 gurdub su$_{11}$-lum
2. 3 gurdub gazi
3. 1 banšur gada
4. 1 gurdub Ú.ḪÁB ḫád

5. me-ság
6. na-bé-a
7. ku-li-mu
8. ù-na-dug$_4$
9. A.IGI.AN.NI-ma-ak
10. il$_8$-at-e-li
11. ama-bára-e ba-na-de$_6$
12. 4 mu 11 iti

Three baskets of dates, three baskets of *wild licorice,* one tray of flax, (and) one basket of dried . . . Thus says Mesag: Tell Kulimu that Ama-barag has taken away . . . *for* Ilat-eli.

Year 4, month 11.

55. ITT 1 1119
(Sumerian)

1. me-ság-e
2. na-bé-a
3. al-la-mu
4. ù-na-dug$_4$
5. a-šà 4 (bùr) GÁNA
6. ḫa-ma-ab-šúm-mu
7. árad-mu-ne
8. [ḫ]é-uru$_4$-n[e]
9. ⌜bar?⌝-bi-da ga-na-ab-⌜ri⌝

Thus says Mesag: Tell Allamu to hand over to me four bur of land, so that my servants can cultivate it. I want to . . .

Sargonic Letters from Elsewhere

An Order for Boats
56. BIN 8 151
(Unknown, Akkadian)

1. *en-ma*
2. ib-ni-LUGAL
3. *a-na da-da*
4. KÙ.GÁL
5. 6 MÁ *ša-at* 30.TA
6. *a-na* pù-BALA
7. *li-dì-in*
8. ma-núm-a-ḫi
9. *si-ip-rí*
10. *li-da-ni-in*

Thus (says) Ibni-sharrum to Dada, the canal inspector: Give Pu-BALA six barges of the 9,000 liter variety. Mannum-ahi should give strict orders (concerning) my instructions!

57. CT 50 69
(Unknown, Akkadian)

1. *[en]-⌈ma⌉*
2. *⌈i⌉-dì-èr-ra*
3. *a-na* al-la-a-bí
4. *da-ni-iš-mì da-ni-iš*
5. *⌈a-ṣí⌉-ḫa-am*
6. 23 ŠE GUR
7. 3 ⌈GÚN⌉ SÍG
8. 2 ⌈DUG⌉ Ì.NUN
9. 5 ⌈DUG⌉ Ì.ŠÁḪ
10. TU.D[A$^?$.M]A.AM
11. *ù* KU$_6$ AB.BA
12. *li-sé-bí-lam*
13. *ù* 30 + [x (iku) GÁ]NA KI.DURU$_5$ SIG$_5$
14. *⌈a-na ḫa⌉-ú-ru$_{14}$*
15. *li-dì-in*

Thus (says) Iddin-Erra to Alla-abi: I was very, very upset! He should bring to me 6,900 liters of grain, three talents of wool, two jars of ghee, five jars of lard, . . . , and sea fish. Moreover, he is to give [x] iku of fine watered land to Ha'uru.

Slaves and Servants

58. CT 50 70
(Unknown, Akkadian)

1. 15 ⌈GÍN⌉ KÙ.BABBAR
2. *en-ma*
3. DINGIR.É
4. *a-na* ì-lí-dan
5. DUMU šu-ga-at
6. u-ra-ì-im^{ki}
7. *ù a-na* du-du
8. 2 SAG-*mì*
9. *aḫ-za-nim*
10. *lu ṣa-aḫ-ra ⌈a⌉ zu-qú-na*
11. *in i-⌈dì⌉ si-ip-ri*
12. *su-rí-a-nim sa-al-la-la*
13. ŠEŠ.MUNUS-*sú ù* a-bù-GIŠ.ÉREN
14. *um-ma-su ù* na-ni
15. *in* SUBIR^{ki}
16. *ba-al-ṭú*

Concerning fifteen shekels of silver. Thus (says) Ili-bitim to Ili-dan, the son of Shugat, of (the city of) Ura'im, and to Dudu: Purchase two slaves for me; they should be young and beardless! Have them sent to me *with my messenger.* (He should know) that Shallala, his sister, and Abu-damiq, his mother, as well as Nani, now live in (the land of) Subartu.

59. CT 50 71
(Unknown, Akkadian)

1. [*en-ma* PN_1]
2. [*a-na* PN_2]
break
1′. 1/2 MA.N[A KÙ.BABBAR]
2′. *iš-*te_4
3′. ma-ba-lum-^{d}da-gan
4′. *im-ḫur*
5′. *en-ma*
6′. qù-ra-dum
7′. *a-na* ú-tá-aḫ
8′. *è-qá-bi*
9′. *at-tá* ÁRAD
10′. *tá-sa-am-ma*
11′. *a-na-*ku_8 6 MU
12′. *ki-iṣ-ri-su*
Rest broken

[Thus (says) so-and-so to so-and-so: . . . so-and-so] has received half a mina of [silver] from Mannum-balum-Dagan. Thus (said) Quradum to Utah: He said as follows: "As for you, you will purchase a/the slave, (and) as for me, [*I will pay you*] for his hire for six years . . .

60. CT 50 86
(Unknown, Akkadian)

1. ⌜1⌝ amar-šuba
2. *in* lagaš⌜^{ki}⌝
3. *u-ša-ab*
4. *li-*⌜*ru-nim*⌝

Amar-shuba is dwelling in Lagash. (Tell) him to send him to me!

Agricultural Matters

61. Westenholz, *JCS* 26:79
(Unknown, Akkadian)

1. *en-*⌜*ma*⌝
2. su-ru-uš-g[i]
3. *a-na* KIL.DINGIR
4. *ù a-na* a-la-li
5. $AŠA_5$ *a ib-ra*
6. ŠE.NUMUN *ù* GUD
7. *in qá-ti-ku-ni*
8. 15 UD *li-im-la-ma*
9. *[in]* ⌜É⌝.^{giš}ŠINIG
10. 1 ḫa-nu-nu
11. 1 rí-ba-tum
12. *li-za-zu-ma*
13. KÁ *ša* ŠE *li-ip-te-u-ma*
14. ŠE.NUMUN ⌜*ù*⌝ ŠE.BA
15. *li-*⌜se_{11}⌝*-ṣí-ù-nim-ma*
16. KÁ *in na-ap-ḫa-rí-su-nu*
17. *li-ik-nu-ku*
18. *mah-rí* i-lu_5-DINGIR ḫa-nu-nu

19. *ù* KIL.DINGIR *ṣa-nam li-ig-zu-zu*
20. 5 MA.NA SÍG *a-na* ḫa-nu-nu
21. *li-dì-nu wa-ar-ki-*⌜*si*⌝*-[in]*
22. X + 10 MA.NA SÍG 4 x [. . .] túgNÍG-[. . .]
23. [X] + 1 túgSA? [x] x SÍG MUG *a-na* MUG ⌜*li?-x*⌝*-ḫa-zu*

Thus (says) Shurush-kin to Kil-dingir and to Alali: Do not let the field remain unworked (lit., hungry)! You have seed-grain and ox(en) at your disposal. Allow fifteen days to pass, appoint Hanunu and Ribatum (for the task) in (the hamlet of) Bit-binim. Have them open the door of the granary (lit., grain), and give out seed grain as well as grain rations, and then they should all (re)seal the door. Hanunu and Kil-dingir should (then) shear the sheep in the presence of Ilu-ilum. They should give five minas of wool to Hanunu. After that for every ten mina of wool, they should weave four . . . garments and they should . . . low quality wool into low quality garments.

62. *JCS* 1:348
(Unknown, Akkadian)

1. *en-ma*
2. tám-tá-lik
3. *a-na* NIMGIR/SAḪAR
4. *qí-bí-* ‹*ma*›
5. 203 ŠE GUR SAG.GÁL
6. mi-su_4-a
7. 143 ŠE GUR
8. i-da-DINGIR
9. ŠU.NÍGIN 346 ŠE GUR SAG.GÁL
10. tá[m-t]á-lik
11. *i[m-ḫ]ur*

Thus (says) Tamtalik: Speak to the herald (or: Mr. NIMGIR, or: Mr. SAHAR): Tamtalik has received a total of 83,040 liters of grain: 48,720 liters of grain (from) Mishu'a (and) 34,320 liters of grain (from) Ida-ilum.

A Quarrelsome Household

63. Veenhof, *JEOL* 24:105
(Unknown, Akkadian)

1. *en-ma*
2. ba-bí
3. *a-na* sa-ar-tim
4. *a-ṣi-ḫa-me*
5. *a-na mi-nim*
6. *at-ti*
7. *ù* i-bí-DINGIR
8. *in* É
9. *tá-ṣa-a-la*
10. *ĩš-te₉-ni-ĩš*
11. *si-ba*
12. Ì.GIŠ *su-bi-lim*

Thus (says) Babi to Shartum: I have been distressed (about you). Why are you quarreling with Ibbi-ilum in the house? Live (in peace) with each other! Send me (some) sesame oil!

64. Donald, *MCS* 9:252
(Unknown, Sumerian)

1. ur-^{d}utu-ke$_4$
2. na-bé-a
3. šeš-šeš-mu
4. ù-na-a-dug$_4$
5. [a]-ga-dè^{ki} lugal-àm
6. lú a-ga-dè^{ki}
7. na-bí-gaz-e
8. ki árad-gi$_4$-gi$_4$-šè
9. lú ḫé-gi$_4$-gi$_4$

Thus says Ur-Utu: Tell my Sheshshesh (or: Sheshsheshmu) that Agade is paramount, that they should not (try to) kill men of Agade and that they should send a messenger to Arad-gigi.

A Request for Salt

65. Neumann, *AoF* 15:210
(Uruk, Sumerian)

1. [lugal]-kalam-e
2. [na]-bé-a
3. [. . .]x KU-ra
4. ⌜ù⌝-na-dug$_4$
5. 2 (UL) mun
6. ḫa-ra-ab-šúm-mu

Seal: lugal-ka[lam] dub-sar
dum[u x?]-É? [. . .]

Thus says Lugal-kalam: Tell . . . -KU to give you 72 liters of salt.

Seal: Lugal-kalam, the scribe,
son of [so-and-so]

Legal Affairs

66. BIN 8 153
(Sumerian)

1. 1 ur-^{d}utu
2. 1 lugal-mas-sú
3. lú DUN-a
4. du-du-me
5. lú di-da
6. ur-lugal-me
7. du-du
8. ù-na-dug$_4$
9. ⌜šu⌝ ḫa-mu-ne-ús-e

Ur-Utu (and) Lugal-masu are the subordinates of Dudu. They are the legal opponents of Ur-lugal. Tell Dudu that he is to dispatch them here.

67. BIN 8 155
(Sumerian)

1. ur-lugal-ke$_4$
2. na-bé-a
3. inim-⌜ma-ra⌝
4. ù-⌜na-dug$_4$⌝
5. 1 nin-x-x
6. 1 x x x
7. lú di-da-mu-me
8. 1 [lu]gal-lú
9. dumu ne-sag
10. 1 ama-sa$_6$
11. 1 ur-gidri
12. dumu á-ni-ta
13. lú ki-inim-ma-me
14. sanga
15. ḫé-na-ab-bé
16. kišib ḫé-ra-ra
17. di-bi di ḫé-bé

Thus says Ur-lugal: Tell [so-and-so] that Nin-. . . and [so-and-so] are my litigants and that Lugallu, son of Nesag, Amasa (and) Ur-gidri, son of Anita are my witnesses. He is to tell this to the chief temple administrator, prepare a sealed document, and press the case to court.

68. BIN 8 157
(Sumerian)

1. ur-[lu]gal-ke$_4$
2. na-bé-a
3. inim-ma-ra
4. ù-na-dug$_4$
5. 1 ur-sipa-da
6. 1 nin-íd-maḫ

7. dam UN-íl
8. nu-èš
9. lú nibru^{ki}-me
10. lú di-da-mu-me
11. nam-maḫ GAR.énsi-ra
12. ḫé-na-ab-bé
13. kišib ḫé-ra-ra
14. di-bi di ḫé-bé

Thus says Ur-lugal: Tell Inima (that) Ur-sipad, Nin-Idmah, as well as the wife of Unil, the neshakku-priest—citizens of Nippur—are my witnesses (and) that Nammah should tell the *city governor* to seal a document, and press the case to court.

Fugitives

69. Yoshikawa, *ASJ* 6:130 (Unknown, Sumerian)

1. [1 PN]
2. dumu nir-DINGIR
3. ugula lugal-e
4. 1 ab-ba
5. 1 ur-^{d}nin-tu
6. ugula en-ni-⸢šè⸣
7. 1 ba-zi
8. 1 lú zàḫ
9. ugula dug-me-lá
10. šu-nígin 5 guruš
12. lú zàḫ-me
13. énsi-ke$_4$
14. na-bé-a
15. šeš-šeš
16. ù-na-dug$_4$
17. en-na-túm
18. é-ÉŠ-ka
19. [. . .]-éš
20. [. . .]

[So-and-so], son of Nir-DINGIR, under the control of Lugale, Abba (and) Ur-Nintu, under the control of Enishe, Bazi (and an unnamed) fugitive, under the control of Dugmela; in total: five young laborers who are fugitives. Thus says the governor: Tell Sheshshesh that Enatum [. . .]ed them in prison. . . .

An Order Concerning Land

70. BIN 8 150
(Unknown, Sumerian)

1. 3 (bùr) GÁNA u_8-e gar-ra
2. ḫa-mu-ra-šúm-ma

(*blank line*)
3. inim-ma-ni-zi

(Tell) him to give you three bur of field *grazed by ewes* (or: the Uegara field).

71. TIM 9 95
(Unknown, Sumerian)

1. na-bé-[a]
2. šeš-šeš-mu
3. ù-na-dug_4
4. 12 gud-giš
5. 1 áb
6. ⌜a⌝-na-lá

Thus says ‹so-and-so›: Tell my Sheshshesh (or: Sheshsheshmu): Twelve draft oxen and one cow have been harnessed for him.

III

Letters from the Time of the Third Dynasty of Ur

Two or three generations after the final fall of the kingdom of Akkad, a new attempt was made to bring Sumer and Akkad under centralized rule. We know very little about the beginnings of the new dynasty except that its original home appears to have been at Uruk. A local king by the name of Utu-hegal, who according to the *Sumerian King List* was the solitary member of the Fourth Dynasty of Uruk, claimed, in one inscription, to have defeated the foreign Gutians and to have restored kingship to Sumer. His reign was brief, perhaps no more than three years. His brother Ur-Namma, who had been the military governor of the city of Ur, seized the opportunity and moved the base of power to his city. By the end of his eighteen-year reign all of Mesopotamia was in the hands of one city again. His son and successor, Shulgi, reigned almost half a century; under his rule the state was consolidated, the eastern and northeastern borders were secured, and the power apparatus was reformed to accommodate the change from city-state to territorial state. Following in the footsteps of Naram-Sin, the fourth king of Akkad, Shulgi pronounced himself a god and ruler of the four corners of the universe. He reformed the army, the relationship between temple and state, as well as the system of taxation, and created a highly centralized bureaucracy to administer the realm. New centers were established to collect taxes in kind from all the provinces of the kingdom. Two such places have been identified, and there may have been more of a similar kind. The first, for the processing of livestock, was located at Puzrish-Dagan, modern Drehem. The second, organized for the collection of grain taxes, was at Dusabara, somewhere in the vicinity of Nippur.

Ur-Namma and his four successors reigned for almost exactly a century (2112–2004 BCE). Their state encompassed Sumer and Babylonia as well as the trade routes to the east—that is, the Diyala valley through the Zagros mountains, the later silk route—as well as the Susiana plain to the south. They set up colonies in the mountain border regions and fought almost unending wars to keep control of the regions flanking the trade routes to the east and northeast. They also established close relationships with border kingdoms—often through diplomatic marriages—and with states as far away as the Mediterranean coast.

The highly specialized bureaucracy of the Ur kingdom left behind one of the largest sets of administrative documents from the ancient world. It is estimated that there are over thirty-four thousand published texts from that period (Sigrist and Gomi 1991); the exact count is difficult to establish as new tablets are constantly being made available. Thousands more lie unpublished in modern museums, and uncounted clay texts remain in the ground in the Near East. That is, of course, only a sample of what was written at the time, and this sample is determined by excavation strategy and by the accidents of discovery. Although we have so many tablets, they come from a relatively small number of ancient cities, primarily from Ur, Puzrish-Dagan, Nippur, Lagash, and Umma, all located in the central and southern parts of the kingdom. Few texts from the north have been found, and the largest such group, from Eshnunna, remains unpublished. With the notable exception of some of the Nippur materials, these texts all come from official archives. That is one of the reasons why we know so little about the private economic activities of the Ur III elites.

The letters from the times of the kings of Ur reflect that distribution of texts. The vast majority are administrative orders, often labeled as letter-orders in the modern literature. Unlike most contemporary administrative documents, letters were rarely dated. Those that have month or year names conform to the standard usage of the day: the years were named after important events of the previous year, or from the beginning of the current year. These names are translated here and explained in terms of regnal years of the kings of Ur. The five kings of this dynasty were: Ur-Namma (18 years, 2112–2095), Shulgi (48 years, 2094–2047), Amar-Sin (8 years, 2046–2038), Shu-Sin (8 years, 2037–2029), and Ibbi-Sin (25 years, 2028–2004).

Royal Affairs

Only a small number of Ur III letters are addressed to or come from the king of the realm. At first glance this may seem quite logical, since one would not expect the king to interfere in small administrative matters of the kind usually referred to in these letters. And yet we have a few letters addressed to "my king," Sumerian lugal-mu. The phrase is ambiguous, since it means "my lord" and therefore, theoretically, could refer to someone of higher status than the sender. The first two letters demonstrate without any doubt that at least some of these messages came to and from the royal chancery. In view of this, the phrase lugal-mu has been rendered here as "His Majesty."

Texts 73 and 74 belong to the correspondence of Ur-Lisi, who was the governor of the southern city and district of Umma, one of the most important strategic posts of the state. Letter 72 is a record of certain deliveries that the governor of Umma had made to the crown during the last three years of Shulgi's reign and in the first year of his successor Amar-Sin. According to Sollberger (1966: 12), the king was not satisfied, and letter 73 is a request for additional deliveries from Ur-Lisi. For other texts concerning the affairs of the Umma governors see letters 98–112.

72. TCS 1 273
(Böhl, *BO* 8, pl. i)

1. ur-^{d}šára-⸢ra⸣
2. ù-na-a-dug_4
3. 1 ma-na kù-babbar
4. mu ki-maš^{ki} ba-ḫul
5. 1/2 ma-na kù-babbar
6. 4 gún 51 2/3 ma-na síg gi
7. sag na_4-bi 8 1/3 ma-na
8. mu ús-sa ki-maš^{ki} ba-ḫul
9. 1 ma-na kù-babbar
10. mu ḫa-ar-ši^{ki} ba-ḫul
11. 1 ma-na kù-babbar
12. mu ^{d}amar-^{d}sìn lugal
13. ki énsi umma^{ki}-⸢ta⸣
14. ^{d}utu-gír-gal
15. šu ba-an-ti
16. gaba-ri mu-de_6-bi

Tell Ur-Shara: Utu-girgal received from the governor of (the city of) Umma:

One mina of silver (during) "the year that Kimash was defeated" (= Shulgi year 46).

One half mina of silver, four talents and 41 2/3 minas of gi wool, the . . . of its stone weights is eight and a third minas, (during) "the year following (the year) that Kimash was defeated (= Shulgi year 47).

One mina of silver (during) "the year that Harshi was defeated (= Shulgi year 48).

One mina of silver (during) "the year that Amar-Sin became king" (Amar-Sin year 1).

(This is) a copy (of the record) of those deliveries.

73. TCS 1 1 (YOS 4 117)

1. lugal-e
2. na-ab-bé-a
3. ur-$^{d}li_9$-si_4-na-ra
4. ù-na-a-dug_4
5. 1/3-ša ḫar kù-babbar
6. 15 túg-ḫi-a
7. 0.0.3 ì du_{10}-ga
8. 0.2.0 ì-giš
9. 1 gud
10. 10 udu máš-ḫi-a
11. lú kin-gi_4-a-gá
12. ḫé-na-ab-šúm-mu

Thus says the king: Tell Ur-Lisi to give my messenger a silver coil (weighing) a third of a mina, 15 assorted garments, 30 liters of good quality oil, 120 liters of sesame oil, one ox, (as well as) 10 assorted sheep and goats.

74. TCS 1 369 (Scheil, *RA* 24:44) (Akkadian)

1. *um-ma šar-ru-um-ma*
2. *a-na* ur-^{d}li$_9$-si$_4$-na
3. *qí-bí-ma*
4. 60.0.0 ŠE GUR
5. *a-na* LÚ.MAḪ
6. *ša* ^{d}INANNA
7. *ša* gír-su^{ki}
8. *i-dì-in*

Thus (says) the king: Speak to Ur-Lisi: Give 18,000 liters of grain to the *lumaḫḫum*-priest of (the goddess) Inanna of Girsu!

75. TCS 1 145 (UET 3 5)

1. lugal-mu
2. ù-na-a-dug$_4$
3. a-ab-[ba]-a
4. amar-šuba-ra
5. níg-gur$_{11}$ ur-gu-[la]-mu-kam
6. a-na a-na-bé-a
7. dub ur-^{d}dumu-zi
8. dumu ur-gu-la-mu
9. šu ti-ti-kam
10. dub šabra-bi in-na-de$_6$-a
11. a-ab-ba-a
12. amar-šuba-ra
13. du$_{11}$-ga-na ì-ni-gi-in

Tell His Majesty: In the matter of what Ajabba had promised Amar-shuba concerning the possessions of Ur-gulamu: The (relevant) document had been taken by Ur-Dumuzi, son of Ur-gulamu. (After) the prefect had brought him the document, he confirmed what Ajabba had promised to Amar-shuba.

76. TCS 1 148 (Diakonoff, *VDI* 1:62)

1. lugal-mu-[r]a
2. ù-na-a-dug$_4$
3. 4 (iku) GÁNA šuku ur-dingir-ra-ka
4. a-šà ka-ma-rí^{ki}-ka
5. ì-in-gál-àm
6. mu ^{d}šu-^{d}sìn lugal-ta
7. lú-^{d}nin-SA.ZA a-zu
8. ba-an-gub
9. kislaḫ-bi-ta
10. 4 (iku) GÁNA a-šà lal-tur
11. ur-dingir-ra-ra
12. lugal-mu in-na-an-šúm
13. a-šà-bi ur-dingir-ra-ke$_4$
14. kin bí-in-na
15. a-šà ús ùnu ù KAM.KAM-ba
16. lú-ib-gal ì-íb-gub
17. lú la-ba-an-da-g[ub]
18. 3 (iku) GÁNA igi lugal-gi-gi-ka
19. ur-dingir-ra-ke$_4$
20. kin bí-in-na
21. ù a-ne-[à]m
22. a ì-in-[d]é

Tell His Majesty: Since the first year of king Shu-Sin, Lu-Nin-SA.ZA, the physician, has occupied the four iku subsistence field of Ur-dingira in the Kamari field. His Majesty (therefore) had given Ur-dingira the four iku Laltur field from its (adjacent) fallow land (and) Ur-dingira has worked this land. (There is another) field, adjoining (the property of) the cowherd(s) and the . . . , which had been occupied by Lu-Ebgal, but which no one was able to occupy (after that); Ur-dingira has worked a three iku (parcel from that land), located in front of (the field) of Lugal-gigi and it is he who has brought water to it (and revived it).

77. TCS 1 149 (TCS 1 pl. 5)

1. lugal-mu-ra
2. ù-na-a-dug$_4$
3. im síg-ba-ke$_4$
4. gù ba-dé
5. šu ḫa-ab-ús-e
6. àga-[uš i]b-g[i$_4$-g]i$_4$
7. gi izi é-šè
8. lú 60-àm
9. gi$_4$-mu-un
10. gi ba-an-tùm am-til

Tell His Majesty to dispatch to me the accounts of the wool rations, as had been promised; have them sent with the constable.

Send me 60 men for the (collecting) of *fire* reeds for the household. Then the reeds will be delivered. That is all.

78. TCS 1 150 = *M.A.R.I.* 5 627

This fragmentary letter would be of little interest, had it not been found in Syria, at the large site of Mari. At this time Mari was an independent state, allied by a diplomatic marriage with the house of Ur from the very beginning, when the daughter of the ruler of the Syrian state married into the family of Ur-Namma. Envoys from Mari, and from other Syrian states such as Urshum, Ebla, and Byblos, regularly visited the court at Ur. It is not certain to whom the letter is addressed, but since it is a typical Ur III letter-order, one may assume that there is some connection with the Sumerian kingdom.

1. lugal-mu-ra
2. ù-na-a-dug$_4$
3. ⌜puzur$_4^?$⌝-[. . .]
4. x [. . .]

Break

1′. éren éren [. . .] ḫé-eb-[. . .]
2′. ⌜e⌝-ma-ru-⌜kam⌝
3′. lugal-mu inim-bi ḫa-mu-tár-re

Tell His Majesty that Puzur-[. .] . . . has . . .
The conscripts . . . It is urgent! (Ask) His Majesty to decide on this matter.

79. BM 20741

1. lugal-mu
2. ù-na-a-dug$_4$
3. 5.0.0 še gur
4. ^{d}utu-kam
5. 5.0.0 še gur
6. lú-^{d}dumu-zi-ra
7. ḫé-na-ab-šúm-mu
8. še-ba UN-íl

Tell my lord to give 1,500 liters of grain to Utukam (and) 1,500 liters of grain to Lu-Dumuzi. (These are) rations for the *menials.*

80. BM 21700

1. [ur]-^{d}lama
2. ⌜ù⌝-na-a-dug$_4$
3. 3.0.0 še gur lugal
4. ur-ki-gu-la lú ázlag
5. hé-na-ba-šúm-mu
6. níg-ba lugal-kam

Tell Ur-Lama to give Ur-kigula, the fuller, 900 liters of grain. It is a royal allotment.

81. TCS 1 312 (TCS 1 pl. 18)

1. šu-^{d}UTU-ra
2. ù-na-a-dug$_4$
3. 10 ^{giš}ù-suḫ$_5$
4. lú kin-gi$_4$-a lú-^{d}en-líl-lá-ke$_4$
5. igi-na ḫé-ni-ib-sa$_6$-ge
6. e$_4$-ma-ru-kam
7. á-ág-g[á] lugal-[kam]
8. na-mi-gu[r-re]

Tell Shu-Shamash to *please* the envoy of Lu-Enlila (by giving him) ten pieces of fir wood. It is urgent! This is the king's instruction! (The matter) must not come up again!

82. TCS 1 130 (TCS 1 pl. 6)

1. lú-^{d}šára
2. ù-na-a-dug$_4$
3. na-ra-ma-da-ad sipa ur-ra
4. šà-gal-ni 2 sìla zíd-ta
5. ḫé-n[a-ab-šúm-m]u
6. ur gi$_7$-[ra]
7. šà-gal níg-gù-dé-bi
8. ḫa-ab-ba-šúm-mu

9. e$_4$-ma-ru-kam
10. inim é-gal-kam
11. inim-gar-bi nu-mu-tùm

Tell Lu-Shara to give Naram-Adad, the dog warden, his food at two liters of flour (per day), and to give him fodder for the dogs, as much as he asks for. It is urgent! This is the order of the Crown! He cannot object to this.

Affairs of the Chancellor

The highest ranking official of the Ur III state after the king was the chancellor, Sumerian sukkal-mah, literally "highest emissary." Arad-Nanna, sometimes called Arad-mu, held this office during the last years of King Shulgi, throughout the reigns of his two sons, and well into the time of the last king of the dynasty, Ibbi-Sin. His father and grandfather had both held this post. The chancellor controlled the military and fiscal affairs of the state and was directly in charge of the eastern part of the state and of many of the border areas in Iran. Arad-Nanna, or his office, sent many if not all the letters to Nani; hence they are included in this section (Lafont 1986: 76). Nani was stationed at Girsu, where he held the title of "chief accountant." There are also later copies of the correspondence of this chancellor with King Shulgi. Copied in Babylonian schools over two hundred years after the fall of the Ur III state, these literary letters provide a glimpse of more complex aspects of political life. Therefore one such epistolary exchange is included here (letters 96 and 97).

83. TCS 1 2 (BM 134634)

1. sukkal-maḫ-e
2. na-bé-a
3. lugal-kù-zu
4. ⌜ù-na⌝-a-dug$_4$
5. é ki-tuš ^{d}⌜nin$^{?}$⌝-é-gal-[la-(ka)]
6. tal a-⌜rá⌝ [x-kam]
7. [ḫé-mi-i]n-si-g[e]
8. [. . .]-àm
9. [. . .]
10. ⌜inim lugal-kam⌝

Thus says the chancellor: Tell Lugal-kuzu to place crossbeams . . . times in the cella of (the temple of the goddess) Nin-egala. . . . It is the order of the king!

84. TCS 1 203 (MVN 11 167)

1. sukkal-mah-ra
2. ù-na-a-dug$_4$
3. di-kuru$_5$ ib-tu-ru-né-eš
4. ù a-ne ib-gub

5. ^{d}šul-gi-re-isiš-ma-an-ág kuš$_7$
6. ù a-bu-DÙG
7. di ù-bí-in-eš
8. lú nam gub-ba tuk-tuku-bi
9. uru-ba giš-a ḫa-in-kéš-e

Tell the chancellor: The judges sat (in court) and he himself was present (there). (Tell) him that after Shulgire-isish-manag, the equerry, and Abu-ṭab present their case, he should conscript as many men as there are available in the city.

85. TCS 1 337 (Gomi—Sato 129)

1. 120.0.0 še gur lugal
2. ^{d}nanna-kam sukkal
3. ki ur-^{d}en-líl-la-ta
4. ba-zi
5. na-ni
6. ù-na-a-dug$_4$
7. ḫé-éb-zi-zi
8. mu si-ma-núm^{ki} ba-ḫul

Seal: ^{d}šu-^{d}sìn
lugal kala-ga
lugal uri$_5$^{ki}-ma
lugal an ub-da límmu-ba
árad-^{d}nanna
sukkal-maḫ
dumu ur-^{d}šul-pa-è
sukkal-maḫ
árad-zu

Ur-Enlila issued 36,000 liters of grain for Nannakam, the messenger. Tell Nani to debit it to him.

The year that Simanum was defeated (= Shu-Sin year 3).

Seal: O Shu-Sin, mighty king, king of Ur, king of the four corners of the universe, Arad-Nanna, the chancellor, the son of Ur-Shulpae, the chancellor, is your servant!

86. TCS 1 230 (BM 25413)

1. ur-^{d}lama-ra
2. ù-na-a-dug$_4$
3. a-šà ^{d}nin-sún-ka-ka
4. ki sa$_6$-ga-bi
5. 4 (bùr) GÁNA
6. nin-ù-numun-e-ki-ág-ra
7. ḫé-na-ra-bar-re
8. inim sukkal-maḫ-kam

Tell Ur-Lama to set aside for Ninu-numune-kiaga four bur of land from the *good part* of the field of the (goddess) Ninsun. It is the chancellor's order!

87. BM 18544

1. na-ni
2. ù-na-a-dug$_4$
3. ^{I}si-gar-kalam-ma
4. ^{I}ur-mes
5. dumu lugal-ka-gi-na-me-éš
6. gìr-sè-ga é ^{d}nin-é-gal-ka šà mar-sa-me-éš
7. na-an-ba-na-a-dù

Tell Nani not to detain Sigar-kalama and Ur-mes, the sons of Lugal-kagina, who are domestics in the temple estate of (the goddess) Ninegala, (working) in the boathouse.

The following two letters give us a rare glimpse of a chain of communications. There is a clear relationship between the two texts; the second text is obviously a follow-up to the first. Babati, who is the central character of these letters, was the uncle of the third and fourth kings of the Ur III dynasty, Amar-Sin and Shu-Sin. He is often encountered in connection with large consignments of grain connected with the central administration of the realm.

88. TCS 1 165 (Gomi—Sato 107)

1. na-ni
2. ù-na-a-dug$_4$
3. dub ba-ba-ti 720.0.0 še gur
4. ur-mes-ra
5. in-da-gál-la
6. šu ḫa-ba-ši-íb-ti
7. ba-ba-ti
8. èn ì-na-tar
9. níg-ŠID-ta ḫa-ni-íb-zi-zi
10. dub ur-mes-a
11. ḫa-ab-zi-ir-re
12. *Erased line that originally read:* na-mi-gur-re

Tell Nani to take over from Ur-mes the account of Babati concerning 216,000 liters of grain. I have asked Babati; let him (Nani) withdraw it from the accounts and destroy the (debt) record of Ur-mes.

Erased line: (The matter) must not come up again!

89. Lafont, *RA* 84:169 no. 2

1. na-ni
2. ù-na-a-dug$_4$
3. dub ba-ba-ti
4. ur-mes-e ì-de$_6$-a-da
5. níg-gibil-gibil-ta
6. lú-en-na dub ur-mes-a
7. in-da-gá-la-a
8. si ḫa-ab-sá-e
9. nam-ma-gi$_4$-g[i$_4$]
10. ba-ba-ti
11. nu-ra-⌜du$_{11}$-ga⌝

Tell Nani: Concerning the tablet of Babati that Ur-mes was to bring: (because) there are new developments in the matter, Lu-enna (now) has the tablet of Ur-mes. (Tell) him to clear up (the matter) and not to come back to me (with the case). Did not Babati speak to you (about this)?

90. TCS 1 177 (TCS 1 pl. 8)

1. na-ni
2. ù-na-a-dug$_4$
3. 60.0.0 še gur
4. e-la-ak-šu-qir-ra
5. ḫé-na-ab-šúm-mu
6. na-mi-gur-re
7. gú-na-kam
8. tukum(ŠU.NÍG.LÁ.TUR)-bi
9. nu-na-an-šúm
10. é-a-ni-ta
11. íb-su-su

Seal: ^{d}šu-^{d}sìn
lugal kala-ga
lugal uri$_5$^{ki}-ma
lugal an ub-da límmu-ba
árad-^{d}nanna
sukkal-maḫ
dumu ur-^{d}šul-pa-è
sukkal-maḫ
árad-zu

Tell Nani to give Ilak-shuqir 18,000 liters of grain. (The matter) must not come up again, as it is part of his obligation! Should he not give it to him, it will be paid back from his own estate!

Seal: O Shu-Sin, mighty king, king of Ur, king of the four corners of the universe, Arad-Nanna, the chancellor, the son of Ur-Shulpae, the chancellor, is your servant!

91. TCS 1 166 (ITT 3 6229)

1. na-ni
2. ù-na-a-dug$_4$
3. kin šuku-ra-šè
4. ur-^{d}ba-Ú-ra
5. é-a-na
6. lú na-ni-⸢ku$_4$⸣-ku$_4$
7. a-na-aš-⸢àm⸣
8. dub-mu ḫé-de$_6$
9. lú ba-an-dù

Tell Nani not to enter the estate of Ur-Ba'u (to press him into) work on subsistence (lands). Why is it that (even though) he carries my tablet, someone has detained him?

92. TCS 1 171 (BM 27833)

1. na-ni
2. ù-na-a-dug$_4$
3. še šà-gal ^{anše}kúnga 0.0.2-ta-bi
4. iti ezen-^{d}d[umu-z]i
5. šu-ba ḫa-ab-⸢ši⸣-íb-gi$_4$-gi$_4$
6. inim lugal-kam

Tell Nani to return the fodder for the equids for the Month of Dumuzi (Lagash month 6 or Umma month 7) at 60 liters each. It is the order of the king!

93. TCS 1 173 (BM 29894)

1. na-ni-ra
2. ù-na-a-dug$_4$
3. 1 šitim-e 3 (iku) GÁNA-àm ḫa-gur$_{10}$-gur$_{10}$
4. 3 (iku) GÁNA-àm ḫa-ab-tab-bé
5. še 3.0.0 gur-àm
6. ḫa-sìg-ge
7. á-ba níg-ŠID ì-ni-ak
8. šu ḫa-bar-re
9. kaskal-šè i-su-bé-eš
10. ^{kuš}a-gá-lá-bi ḫa-kéš-e

Tell Nani to have each builder harvest three iku of land, *pile up* (*grain-stacks*) on three iku of land, (and) thresh 900 liters of grain. (Tell) him to release them (after) having settled the account(s) of their wage(s), (and) to prepare their provisions (lit., tie their leather bags) (so that) they can go on their way (home) [or: they can go on the expedition].

94. TCS 1 182 (TCS 1 pl. 8)

1. na-ni
2. ù im-ti-dam-ra
3. ù-na-a-dug$_4$
4. 1.0.0 ì-giš gur
5. ú-tù-ul-é-a
6. ḫé-na-ab-šúm-mu-e
7. lú kin-gi$_4$-a-ka-ni ḫé-em-da-de$_6$

Tell Nani and Imtidam to give Utul-Ea 300 liters of sesame oil. (Tell him) to have his messenger take it.

95. TCS 1 50 (BM 25354)

1. da-a-mu
2. ù ur-^{d}lama-ra
3. ù-ne-a-dug$_4$
4. šu-ku$_8$-bu-um

5. sukkal-maḫ-e
6. ki šuku-a-ni
7. nu-me-a 1 (èše) GÁNA
8. in-na-an-šúm
9. gá-e maškim-šè
10. ì-tuku

Tell Da'amu and Ur-Lama that Shu-kubum, to whom the chancellor had given a field of one eshe because he had no subsistence (field), has taken me for (his) bailiff (in the court case).

96. Arad-mu to Shulgi No. 1

1. lugal-mu-ra ù-na-a-dug$_4$
2. ^{I}árad-mu árad-zu na-ab-bé-a
3. kur su-bir$_4$^{ki}-šè ḫar-ra-an kaskal si sá-sá-e-ra
4. gún ma-da-zu ge-en-ge-né-dè
5. a-rá ma-da zu-zu-dè
6. ugu a-pi-il-la-ša gal-zu unken-na-šè
7. ad-gi$_4$-gi$_4$-dè gù-téš-a sì-ge-dè
8. KA.UD.DA ka-ne-ne-a ḫé-en-tùm á-šè mu-e-da-a-ág
9. ká é-gal-la-šè gub-a-mu-dè
10. silim-ma lugal-gá-ke$_4$ èn li-bí-in-tar
11. tuš na-ma-ta-an-zi ki-a nu-ub-za
12. ba-an-da-mud-dè-en
13. te-gá-e-da-mu-dè
14. é kaskal-la-zu ga-rig$_7$-a$_5$ dálla kù-sig$_{17}$ kù-babbar
15. ^{na4}gug ^{na4}za-gìn gar-ra-ta a-ab-dù-dù-a 30 sar-àm i-íb-tuš
16. kù-sig$_7$ ^{na4}za-gìn-na mí zi-dè-eš im-me
17. ^{giš}gu-za bára šutur-e ri-a i-íb-tuš
18. ^{giš}gìri-gub kù-sig$_{17}$-ga-ka gìri-ni i-íb-gar
19. gìri-ni na-ma-ta-an-kúr
20. àga-uš sag-gá-na 5 li-mu-um-ta-àm zi-da gùb-bu-na íb-ta-an-gub-bu-uš
21. 6 gud niga 60 udu niganíg-zú-gub-šè in-gar
22. šu-luḫ lugal-gá-ke$_4$ sá bí-in-dug$_4$
23. ká-na èn nu-tar-ra-bi lú na-ba-ši-in-ku$_4$-re-en
24. ku$_4$-ku$_4$-da-mu-dè
25. ^{giš}gu-za gàr-ba kù-sig$_{17}$ ḫuš-a gar-ra lú ma-an-túm tuš-a ma-an-dug$_4$
26. á-ág-gá lugal-gá-ke$_4$ ì-gub-bé-en nu-tuš-ù-dè-en bí-dug$_4$
27. 2 gud niga 20 udu niga ^{giš}banšur-mu lú ma-an-di
28. nu-kár-kár-da àga-uš lugal-gá-ke$_4$ ^{giš}banšur-mu in-bal-a-šè
29. ní ba-da-te su ba-da-zi
30. iti ezen-^{d}nin-a-zu u$_4$ 5-àm zal-la-àm

31. lugal-mu á-še mu-e-da-a-ág
32. iti u$_5$-bí-gu$_7$ u$_4$ 1-àm zal-la-àm
33. ^{lú}kas$_4$-e mu-ši-in-gi$_4$
34. iti sa$_9$-àm x-e ba-te
35. lugal-mu ḫé-en-zu

To my lord speak: Thus says Arad-mu, your servant:

You instructed me to take the road to Subir to put in order the provincial taxes, to inform (me) of the state of the provinces, to counsel and come to an agreement with Apillasha, the high commissioner, . . .

When I stood at the gate of his palace no one inquired about the well-being of my lord. The one who was sitting did not rise, did not bow down, (and) *I became nervous.* When I came nearer, (I discerned that) in your expedition house combs and pins inlaid with gold, silver, carnelian, and lapis-lazuli had been set up; they covered an area of 30 sar! (Apillasha himself) was decked out in gold and lapis-lazuli. He sat on a throne which was set up on a high-quality cloth cover (and) had his feet set on a golden footstool. He would not remove his feet in my presence. Choice troops, five thousand strong, stood to his right and left. (He ordered) six grass-fed oxen and 60 grass-fed sheep placed (on the tables) for a meal; the lustrations for my king were performed. At the gate at which I had not been greeted a man bade me to enter.

After I came in, a man brought me a chair with a knob encrusted with red gold and told me, "Sit down!" I answered him: "When I am on the order(s) of my king I stand—I do not sit!" Someone brought me two grass-fed oxen and 20 grass-fed sheep for my table. Although I had not (even) *flinched,* my king's troops overturned my table! I was terrified, I was in fear (for my life)!

At the end of the fifth day of the Month of the Festival of Ninazu (Drehem month 5 or Ur month 6) His Majesty provided me with instructions. (Now) the first day of the Month of the Eating of the Ubi-Bird (Drehem month 3 or Ur month 4) has passed a messenger has returned (to you). Half a month . . . *approaches.* May my king know!

97. Shulgi to Arad-mu No. 1

1. árad-mu-ra ù-na-a-dug$_4$
2. ^{d}šul-gi lugal-zu na-ab-bé-a
3. lú in-ši-gi$_4$-in-na-zu lú DUN-a-zu in-nu-ù
4. šu-zu-ta-àm á-ág-gá šu la-ba-ra-ab-te-gá-e
5. a-na-aš-àm níg-a-na an-ga-àm bí-in-ak-ni ur$_5$ ì-me-a nu-e-zu
6. gá-e níg gá-e-gin$_7$-nam ma-da ge-né-dè
7. un si sá-sá-e-dè suḫuš ma-da ge-en-ge-né-dè
8. uru ma-da ba-te-gá-dè-en-na-zu umuš-bi zu-zu-a

9. lú gal-gal-bé-ne inim-bi zu-àm
10. za-pa-ág-mu kur-kur ḫé-eb-si
11. á kala-ga á nam-ur-sag-gá-mu kur-re ḫé-en-šub-šub
12. u$_{17}$-lu-mu kalam-ma ḫé-eb-dul
13. sìg-sìg eden-na bad$_{5}$-bad$_{5}$ a-šà-ga ú-gu dé-ni-ib
14. en-na a-pi-la-ša gal-zu-unken-na sá an-né-en
15. igi-zu è-ni-ib igi-zu ḫé-en-ši-ku$_{4}$
16. á-šè mu-e-da-a-ág
17. a-na-aš-àm gá-gin$_{7}$-nam nu-un-ak
18. tukum-bi gal-zu-unken-na-mu gá-a-gin$_{7}$-nam nu-ub-gur$_{4}$
19. ^{giš}gu-za bára šutur-e ri-a nu-ub-tuš
20. ^{giš}gìri-gub kù-sig$_{17}$-ka gìri-ni nu-ub-gar
21. énsi nam-énsi-ta
22. lú PA.LUGAL nam-PA.LUGAL-ta
23. ní-te-ní-te-a li-bí-ib-gar ù nu-ub-ta-gub-bu
24. lú nu-un-gaz igi nu-un-ḫul
25. lú igi-bar-ra-ka-ni lú-a li-bí-in-diri
26. a-na-gin$_{7}$-nam ma-da íb-gi-ne
27. tukum-bi ki um-mu-e-a-ág
28. šà-zu šà-ka-kešda ba-ra-na-gá-gá
29. ì-gur$_{4}$-re-en àga-uš-zu nu-e-zu
30. nam-lú-u$_{17}$-lu-bi ù nam-ur-sag-gá-mu igi-zu bí-in-zu
31. tukum-bi emedu-mu za-e-me-en-zé-en
32. igi mìn-na-zu-ne-ne-a im-sar-ra gù ḫé-em-ta-dé-dé-ne
33. gù-téš-a sì-ke-dè-en-zé-en
34. suḫuš ma-da ge-né-dè-en-zé-en
35. e$_{4}$-ma-ru-kam

To Arad-mu speak: Thus says Shulgi, your lord:

That man whom you have sent to me, he cannot (really) be your trusted subordinate! Surely he does not take his orders from your hand! How is it that you are unaware of what he is doing? You were to make fast the territories as if you were me; you were to make safe the people and keep them obedient. After you had arrived in the citi(es) of the territory you were to discern their plan(s). Their (local) dignitaries know their orders! My roar is to cover the land(s); my strong weapon, my heroic weapon is to subdue the foreign lands; my storm is to cover the land!

Avoid attack on the steppe and defeat in the open field, until you have reached Apillasha, my high commissioner, . . . ! Thus I instructed you—why is it that you have not done so?

If my high commissioner had not elevated himself as if he were me, if he had not sat down on a throne set on a quality cloth (cover), if he had not set his feet on a golden footstool, had not by his own authority appointed and removed governors from the office of city governor, royal officers from the position of royal officer, had not killed or blinded anyone, had not elevated, by his own authority, those of his own choice (to positions of power)—how else could he have maintained order in the territory?

If you (truly) love me you will not set your heart on anger! You have made yourself too important, you do not know your (own) soldiers! Be aware of (the power) of your own men and of my *might!*

If you are (indeed) both my loyal servants, you will both listen carefully to my message. Both of you—come to an understanding; make fast the foundation of the land! It is urgent!

Affairs of the Governor of Umma

Umma was one of the important central districts of Sumer. It was never officially excavated, but sometime during the first decade of this century it was plundered of tens of thousands of cuneiform tablets. The city was a major supplier of wood and reed materials, animal products, and grain. It was of strategic importance as a staging area for military expeditions, diplomatic missions, and regular postal contact with southwestern Iran. Much of the Ur III documentation from Umma must come from the central offices of the governors appointed by the Crown. Although many of the preserved texts include the seals of the governors themselves, it is obvious that this was only a legitimating device and that certain officials had the right to roll the governor's seal on tablets. There is even evidence that there existed multiple copies of these seals. Thus, the letters in this group should perhaps be ascribed to the central chancellery rather than to the person of the governor.

One of the important industries of Umma was the harvesting of the reed thickets and brush forests in the vicinity of the city. The organization of this industry has been recently discussed by Steinkeller (1987). Because some of the letters concerning reeds and wood products were sealed by the governor and his officials, other texts concerning these materials are also included in this section.

98. TCS 1 236 (BM 107681)

1. ur-^{d}li$_{9}$-si$_{4}$-ra
2. ù-na-a-dug$_{4}$
3. é kù-^{d}šára-ka
4. lugal-e šu in-na-ba
5. šu ḫ̮é-ba-re

Tell Ur-Lisi to release the estate of Ku-Shara; the king has (already) released it to him.

99. TCS 1 190 (YOS 4 142)

1. ni$_9$-gar-ki- ‹dùg›
2. ù-na-a-dug$_4$
3. 0.1.0 še ‹gur› lugal
4. šà-gal sila$_4$ kin-gi$_4$- ‹a› -šè
5. uš-mu
6. hé-na-ab-šúm-mu
7. dub-ba-ni šu ha-ba- ‹ši› -íb-ti
8. šà bal-a

Seal: ^{d}šul-gi
nita kala-ga
lugal uri$_5$^{ki}-ma
lugal an ub-da límmu-ba

ur-^{d}li$_9$-si$_4$
énsi
umma^{ki}
árad-zu

Tell Nigar-kidug to give Ushmu 60 royal ‹liters› of grain as fodder for the lambs (whose internal organs will be used for taking) omens. (Tell him) to receive his receipt: it is from the *regular* obligations.

Seal: O Shulgi, mighty man, king of Ur, king of the four corners of the universe—Ur-Lisi, governor of Umma, is your servant!

100. BM 130705

1. lugal-nisag-e
2. ù-na-a-dug$_4$
3. 60 (sìla) zú-lum
4. ur-^{d}sìn
5. ḫé-na-ab-šúm-mu
6. na-mi-gur-re
7. še-bi ga-an-na-ab-šúm-mu

Seal: ur-^{d}li$_9$-si$_4$
énsi
umma^{ki}

a-da-ga
dub-sar
árad-zu

Tell Lugal-nisage to give Ur-Sin 60 liters of dates. (The matter) must not come up again; I will give him its equivalent in grain.

Seal: O Ur-Lisi, governor of Umma—Adaga, scribe, is your servant.

101. Touzalin, Administration 52

1. 180 sa ^{giš}ma-nu
2. 180 sa gi
3. lú-^{d}nanna
4. ḫé-na-ab-šúm-mu
5. gìri lugal-zimbir^{ki}

Seal: ^{d}šul-gi | ur-^{d}li$_9$-si$_4$
nita kala-ga | énsi
lugal uri$_5$^{ki}-ma | umma^{ki}
lugal an ub-da límmu-ba | árad-zu

(Tell) him to give Lu-Nanna 180 bundles of *willow* wood and 180 bundles of reeds. The comptroller is Lugal-Zimbir.

Seal: O Shulgi, mighty man, king of Ur, king of the four corners of the universe—Ur-Lisi, governor of Umma, is your servant!

102. MVN 14 465

1. 120 sa gi
2. maš-gu-la-ra
3. ḫé-na-ab-šúm-mu
4. ka íd-ÍB.TÙR^{ki}-ka

Seal: ^{d}šu-^{d}sin | a-a-kal-la
lugal kala-ga | énsi umma^{ki}
lugal uri$_5$^{ki}-ma | árad-zu
lugal an ub-da límmu-ba

(Tell) him to give Mashgula 120 bundles of reeds at the opening of the Ibtur canal.

Seal: O Shu-Sin, mighty king, king of Ur, king of the four corners of the universe—Aja-kala, governor of Umma, is your servant!

103. Parr, *JCS* 24:136

1. lugal-nanga
2. ù-na-a-dug$_4$
3. 300 sa gi
4. šu-^{d}sìn-ra
5. ḫé-na-ab-šúm-mu
6. na-mi-gur-re

Seal: ^{d}amar-^{d}sìn | ur-^{d}li$_9$-si$_4$
nita kalaga | énsi
lugal uri$_5$^{ki}-ma | umma^{ki}
lugal an ub-da límmu-ba | árad-zu

Tell Lugal-nanga to give (prince?) Shu-Sin 300 bundles of reeds. (The matter) must not come up again!

Seal: O Amar-Sin, mighty man, king of Ur, king of the four quarters of the universe—Ur-Lisi, governor of Umma, is your servant!

104. MVN 3 353

1. 40 sa gi
2. a-gu-ti
3. ḫé-na-ab-šúm-mu

Seal

4. dub a-kal-la
5. ba-an-na-a šu ba-ti

Seal: a-kal-la
dub-sar
dumu ur-nigar^gar kuš$_7$

(Tell) Aguti to give him 40 bundles of reeds.

Seal: Aja-kala, scribe, son of Ur-nigar, the equerry.

Subscript: Bannaja has received the tablet of Aja-kala.

105. Cooper, *JCS* 35:197

1. [lug]al-á-zi-da
2. ù-na-a-dug$_4$
3. 70 sa gi
4. ur-é-diri-ra
5. ḫé-na-ab-šúm-mu
6. ù ‹a?›-ne ḫé-em-da-de$_6$

Tell Lugal-azida to give 70 bundles of reeds to Ur-ediri (and tell) him (i.e., Ur-ediri) to bring them to me.

106. Peat, *JCS* 28:1

1. šeš-a-ni
2. ù-na-a-dug$_4$
3. 30 sa gi
4. a-rá-mu
5. ḫé-na-ab-⌜šúm⌝-mu

Tell Sheshani to give Aramu 30 bundles of reeds.

107. MVN 14 23

1. 5 ^giš^kid má
2. lugal-e-ba-an-sa$_6$-ra
3. ḫé-na-ab-šúm-mu

Seal: lugal-ezen dub-sar
dumu lugal-é-maḫ-e
ša[bra]

(Tell) him to give Lugale-bansa two reed mats for a boat.

Seal: Lugal-ezen, scribe, son of Lugal-Emahe, the prefect.

108. YOS 15 98

1. šeš-a-ni
2. ù-na-a-dug$_4$
3. 30 sa gi
4. lugal-e-ba-an-sa$_6$
5. ḫa-mu-na-ab-šúm-mu

Tell Sheshani to give Lugale-bansa 30 bundles of reeds.

109. Touzalin, Administration 92

1. 90 sa gi
2. ad-da-gu-la
3. 60 sa kù-ga-ni
4. 30 sa nam-ḫa-ni
5. na-mi-gú-re

Seal: lugal-ezen dub-sar
dumu lugal-é-maḫ-e
šabra

(Tell him to give) 90 bundles of reeds to Adda-gula, 60 bundles to Kugani, (and) 30 to Namhani. (The matter) must not come up again!

Seal: Lugal-ezen, scribe, son of Lugal-Emahe, the prefect.

110. Touzalin, Administration 44

1. 30 sa ^{giš}ma-[nu]
2. ḫa-mu-na-šúm

(Tell) him to give (the bearer) 30 bundles of *willow* wood.

111. Touzalin, Administration 47

1. 3 gún gi
2. lú ki-tuš-lú-ra
3. ḫé-na-ab-šúm-mu

Seal: árad-mu
dub-sar
dumu ur-nigar^{gar}

(Tell) him to give three talents of reeds to the man of Kitushlu.

Seal: Arad-mu, scribe, son of Ur-nigar.

112. MVN 15 249

1. 100 sa gi
2. 100 sa ^{giš}ma-nu
3. ki-ága ì-rá-rá-ra ḫé-na-ab-šúm-mu
4. iti min èš mu an-⸢ša⸣-‹an› ^{ki} ba-ḫul

Seal: ur-^{d}šára
dub-sar
dumu lugal-nanga
nu-bànda gud ^{d}šára

(Tell so-and-so) to give Kiaga, the perfumer, 100 bundles of reeds and 100 bundles of *willow* wood. Month Minesh (= Drehem month 1, Ur month 2), the year that Anshan was defeated (= Shulgi year 34).

Seal: Ur-Shara, scribe, son of Lugal-nanga, inspector of the herds of (the god) Shara.

Affairs of the Governor of Nippur

Nippur was one of the most important cities of Sumer because it was the cult center of the most important deity in the land, Enlil. Even though Nippur never held political hegemony, it was an ideological capital, and all rulers who had pretensions of dominion over Sumer paid homage to Enlil in his temple Ekur. During the Ur III period a succession of governors ruled the city, including at least three members of a powerful local family that controlled many high offices in the temples of Enlil and Inanna, as well as in city government (Hallo 1972; Zettler 1984).

113. Owen, AOAT 22 131

1. ur-nigar-mu
2. ù ur-sukkal
3. ù-na-a-dug$_4$
4. [g]ud á-la-la
5. šu ḫé-bar-re

Seal: [d]šu-^{d}sin
ki-ága ^{d}en-líl-lá
lugal kala-ga
lugal uri$_5$^{ki}-ma
lugal an ub-da límmu-ba
nam-z[i-tar-ra]
énsi
nibru^{ki}
dumu ur-^{d}nanibgal
énsi
nibru^{ki}-ka
árad-[zu]

Tell Ur-nigarmu and Ur-sukkal that they are to release the ox of Alala.

Seal: O Shu-Sin, beloved of (the god) Enlil, mighty king, king of Ur, king of the four corners of the universe—Namzitara, governor of Nippur, son of Ur-Nanibgal, governor of Nippur, is your servant!

114. TCS 1 73 (Ni 372)

1. ḫa-ba-lu$_5$-ke$_4$-ra
2. ù-na-a-dug$_4$
3. ur-sukkal-ka
4. lú-bí-bí
5. si ḫa-mu-sá-dè
6. inim-bi di ḫé-bé

Seal: ^{d}šu-^{d}sìn
lugal kala-ga
lugal uri$_5$^{ki}-ma
lugal an ub-da límmu-ba
nam-zi-tar-ra
dumu ur-^{d}nanibgal
énsi
nibru^{ki}-ka
árad-zu

Tell Habaluke to arbitrate between Ur-sukkal and Lu-bibi, (and) press their matter to court.

Seal: O Shu-Sin, mighty king, king of Ur, king of the four corners of the universe, Namzitara, the son of Ur-Nanibgal, governor of Nippur, is your servant!

115. TCS 1 61 (TMH 1/2 351)

1. é-a-ba-ni
2. ù-na-a-dug$_4$
3. 1 èr-ra-ga-ši-ir
4. dumu nibru^{ki}-kam
5. ur-sa$_6$-ga
6. ḫa-mu-na-šúm-mu

Envelope

Seal: ^{d}i-bí-^{d}sìn
dingir kalam-ma
lugal kala-ga
lugal uri$_5$^{ki}-ma
lugal an ub-da límmu-ba
da-da
énsi
nibru^{ki}
dumu ur-^{d}nanibgal
énsi
nibru^{ki}-ka
árad-zu

Tell Ea-bani to hand over to Ur-saga one Erra-gashir, a citizen of Nippur.

Envelope
Seal: O Ibbi-Sin, god of the land, mighty king, king of Ur, king of the four quarters of the universe—Dada, governor of Nippur, son of Ur-Nanibgal, governor of Nippur, is your servant!

Prisoners, Fugitives, and Robbers

116. TJAMC 57

1. zàḫ ú-šè-⌜ḫé⌝-gin
2. zàḫ la-ni
3. šeš ur-sa$_6$-ga
4. ⌜énsi⌝ en-na ì-gin-na-aš
5. min-a-bi en-nun-ga ḫé-ti
6. inim énsi-ka
7. a-kal-la šeš unken-né
8. ur-sukka[l še]š lú-kal-la
9. ^{d}[utu$^?$]-mu
10. dumu ur-nigar šu-i
11. uru ḫé-mi-ni-tuš

Escapee: Ushe-hegin.
Escapee: Lani, brother of Ur-saga.
Until the governor has arrived, both of them are to stay in jail. It is the order of the governor!
Aja-kala, brother of Unkene; Ur-sukkal, brother of Lu-kala; and Utu-mu, son of Ur-nigar, the barber, are to remain in the city!

117. NATN 1

1. amar-šuba
2. ù-na-a-dug$_4$
3. lugal-engar$^{?}$
4. ^{d}en-líl-lá
5. dumu-bi
6. tum-al
7. al-šú-ge-eš
8. šu ḫé-ba-⌜re⌝

Seal: ^{d}en-líl-gin$_7$
dub-sar
dumu ur-gu

Tell Amar-shuba to release Lugal-engar and his son Enlila, who are are living in the Tummal (precinct).

Seal: Enlilgin, scribe, son of Urgu.

118. Owen, *Or*NS 40:398 (Akkadian)

1. *a-na* i-ri-dan
2. *ù* DINGIR-ra-bí
3. *q[ì]-bi-ma*
4. *me-nu-um* DINGIR-ra-bí
5. KÙ.BABBAR 1 MA.NA
6. *a-na* lú-^{d}inanna
7. *me-nu-um la ĩš-qú-ul*
8. *i-na ṣí-bi-ti-im*
9. *na-dì-a-ku*
10. *šu-ip-ra-am lu-de$_6$-e*

Speak to Iridan and Ili-rabi: Why, oh why, has Ili-rabi not paid (*back*) Lu-Inanna the mina of silver? I am being jailed (because of this matter)! Write to me so that I may know (what is going on)!

119. TCS 1 6 (Kraus, *BO* 15:77-78)

1. 1 a-tu
2. 1 lú-urub$_x$(URU × KÁR)^{ki}
3. 1 lugal-má-[gur$_8$-re]
4. lú sa-gaz-m[e]
5. [bára-s]i$_{11}$-ga^{ki}-a
6. [ì]-durun$_x$(TUŠ.TUŠ)-éš
7. [g]ala-e
8. na-a[b-bé-a]
9. ur-[. . .]
10. ù-[na-(a)-dug$_4$]
11. ⌜énsi⌝-ra
12. ḫé-na-ab-šúm-mu

Atu, Lu-Urub, (and) Lugal-magure are robbers, they are being held (lit., staying) in (the town of) Barasiga. Thus says the cantor: Tell Ur- . . . to give them to the city governor.

120. TCS 1 196 (TrDr 67)

1. nu-bànda
2. ù-na-a-dug_4
3. 64 udu
4. udu ur-mes
5. éren-e
6. a-[giš]geštin-dílim-ka
7. ì-íb-dab_5
8. é-$duru_5$
9. lú-àra-ka-šè
10. mu im_4-la-ḫe-šè
11. igi árad-[d]nanna-šè
12. igi lú-gi-na-šè
13. udu še gu_7-a-aš
14. ba-gi-in
15. èn ḫé-tar-re

Tell the captain: Conscripts took 64 sheep belonging to Ur-mes from the Ageshtindilim (field). It has been confirmed that while they were being driven toward the hamlet of Lu-ara, (these) sheep grazed within the sight of Arad-Nanna and Lu-gina. (Tell him) to investigate (this matter)!

Letters, Envelopes, and Receipts

Most of the Ur III letters are simple orders requesting that the recipient perform an action. An order would arrive encased in an envelope. The recipient would break open the sealed covering, read the instructions, and perform the task that was required. Often this would require a receipt, and in some cases a new envelope was fashioned around the tablet with the original letter, inscribed with the receipt, and sealed by the issuing agent. There are only two unequivocal instances of this practice, but one cannot rule out that many more letters are hidden inside unopened receipts. The third example below may exemplify a slightly different bureaucratic practice, but translation difficulties preclude a definitive evaluation of the relationship between the text of the tablet and that of the envelope.

Many letters undoubtedly had the address written on the envelope. Only one such example has survived, and it was preserved only because a small portion of the covering clay was stuck to the tablet (no. 126).

121. Owen, *JCS* 24:134

Envelope:

1. 95.0.0 še gur lugal
2. ki DINGIR-*ba-ni* šabra-ta
3. šu-[d]IŠKUR $kuš_7$
4. šu ba-ti
5. šà é [d]šára-ka

Seal: šu-^{d}IŠKUR
kuš$_7$ lugal
dumu ga-mi-lum

Tablet:

1. ḫé-sa$_6$-ra
2. ù-na-a-dug$_4$
3. 95.0.0 še gur
4. šà é ^{d}šára-ka
5. šu-^{d}adad-ra
6. ḫé-na-ab-šúm-mu
7. na-mi-gur-re

Envelope: Shu-Adad, the equerry, received 28,500 liters of grain from the prefect Ilum-bani from/in the temple of (the god) Shara.

Seal: Shu-Adad, royal equerry, son of Gamilum.

Tablet: Tell Hesa to give Shu-Adad 28,500 liters of grain from/in the temple of (the god) Shara. (The matter) must not come up again!

122. Van De Mieroop, *OLP* 15:56

Envelope:

1. 2 gún 47 ma-na bappir
2. [ki]šib ur-nigar^{gar}
3. ki lú-bi-mu-ta

Seal: ur-nigar$^{⌜gar⌝}$
dumu ur-^{d}bì[l-ga-mes]
sipa udu [x x$^{?}$]

Tablet:

1. ur-nigar^{gar}-ra
2. ù-na-a-dug$_4$
3. 2 gún 47 ma-na bappir
4. si-ì-tum
5. lú-bi-mu
6. kišib ḫé-na-ab-ra-ra

Envelope: Two talents and 47 minas of beer-cakes from Lubimu, under Ur-nigar's seal.

Seal: Ur-nigar, son of Ur-Bilgames, shepherd of the . . . sheep.

Tablet: Tell Ur-nigar to make out a sealed document (lit., to roll the seal for him) for two talents and 47 minas of beer-cakes as the arrears of Lubimu.

123. TCS 1 83 (MVN 6 175 = ITT 4 7178)

Envelope:

1. 6 gud še sumun ba-an-sa_{10}-a
2. 2 gud lá-u_x(NI) še g[ibil-ka]
3. ki sanga [^{d}gá-túm-dùg-ta]
4. a[pin-na ba-an-si-a]
5. mu ús-s[a bàd ma-da ba-dù]
6. ki ka_{10}-mu-šè

Seal: ur-^{d}[. . .]
dub-[sar]
dumu ur-^{d}en-líl-[lá]

Tablet:

1. ka_{10}-mu
2. ù-na-a-dug_4
3. 2 gud lá-u_x(NI) še gibil-ka
4. 6 gud še sumun im-ma-ta-sa_{10}-a
5. ki sanga ^{d}gá-túm-dùg-ta
6. apin-na ba-an-si
7. mu ús-sa bàd ma-da ba-dù

Envelope: Six oxen purchased with the old grain (crop), and two oxen (accounted for) from the arrears of the new grain (crop), yoked to the plow *by* (or: from the account of) the chief administrator of (the temple of the goddess) Gatumdug.

The year after (the year that) the wall of the land was built (= Shulgi year 38).

By authority of Kamu.

Seal: Ur-. . . , scribe, son of Ur-Enlila.

Tablet: Tell Kamu: Two oxen (to be accounted for) from the arrears of the new grain (crop, and) six oxen that he will purchase (or: has purchased) with the old grain (crop) are *to be* yoked to the plow *by* (or: from the account of) the chief administrator of (the temple of the goddess) Gatumdug.

The year after (the year that) the wall of the land was built (= Shulgi year 38).

124. Michalowski, *JCS* 28:168

Tablet:

1. ur-^{d}bíl-ga-mes
2. ⸢ù⸣-na-a-dug_4
3. [x] še gur
4. [x] sa_{10}-sa_{10}-dè

5. [pu]zur$_4$-^{d}šára
6. [ḫ̮é]-na-ab-šúmu
7. gá-⌜e⌝
8. ⌜uri⌝$_5$^{ki}-⌜ma⌝
9. ga-⌜na⌝-ág

Envelope:

ur-^{d}b[ìl]-ga-mes [šà$^{?}$] u[ri$_5$]^{ki}-[ma$^{?}$]

Seal: [^{d}i]-bí-[^{d}s]ìn
[nita ka]la-ga
[lugal an ub-da límmu]-ba
[PN]
d[am$^{?}$-gàr]
[árad-zu]

Tell Ur-Bilgames to give Puzur-Shara x liters of grain to purchase . . . . I myself will measure it out for him in Ur (when I come there).

Envelope: Ur-Bilgames, in Ur.

Seal: O Ibbi-Sin, mighty man, king of the four corners of the universe, [so-and-so], the merchant(?), [is your servant]!

The Affairs of Women

Control of writing in ancient Mesopotamia was directly related to the hierarchies of power in society. It is therefore hardly surprising that the affairs of women are not commonly mentioned in official texts from these patriarchal societies. Although some women, particularly those of high birth, were active in economic and political affairs, the majority of women from the middle levels of society were defined by the roles of their husbands, fathers, and brothers.

125. TCS 1 25 (ITT 3 6176)

1. al-la-mu
2. ù-na-a-dug$_4$
3. 1/3-ša kù-babbar íd-da šub-a
4. ur-nigar^{gar}
5. ù dam lú-ba-ra
6. ḫ̮é-éb-lá-e
7. ud na-bí-zal-e
8. ba-ḫ̮a-ra-am-⌜ta⌝-ra
9. ḫ̮é-na-ab-šúm-mu

Tell Allamu to pay (back) to Ur-nigar and the wife of Luba the one third of a mina of silver that was *thrown away* (lit., thrown in the canal)! (Tell him) that not (even) a day must pass, that he must give (the silver) to Baharamta!

126. TCS 1 46 (TCS 1 pl. 2)

1. ba-lu$_5$-lu$_5$
2. ù-na-a-dug$_4$
3. dam gu-za-ni-ra
4. šu ḫa-bar-re
5. na-mi-gur-re

Tell Balulu to release the wife of Guzani. (The matter) must not come up again!

127. TCS 1 54 (ITT 3 6511)

1. dam ur-[^{d}ba-Ú-ka-ra]
2. ù-na-a-du[g$_4$]
3. ur-^{d}ba-Ú x [x$^?$] lú-^{d}nin-šubur munu$_4$-m[ú]
4. šeš-mu bar-mu-a
5. šu ḫa-mu-bar-e
6. e-ne-àm inim en-nu-gá-[ta$^?$] ma-an-dab$_5$
7. šabra lú k[in]-gi$_4$-[a-mu]
8. nam-mi-gu[r-re]
9. a-ba ama-[mu-gin$_7$]

Tell the wife of Ur-[Ba'u] that Ur-Ba'u, the . . . , is to release the maltster Lu-Ninshubur, my brother, on my responsibility. (Tell her that) it was he (Ur-Ba'u) who detained him for me by command of the prison (warden) on my behalf. The prefect is my messenger. (The matter) must not come up again! Who is (as good) as my mother?

128. TCS 1 74 (BM 87135)

1. ḫa-lí-mu
2. ù-na-a-dug$_4$
3. dam ú-da-na
4. a-kal-la-ra
5. šu-du$_8$-a-[šè ḫa]-na-šúm-mu

Tell Halimu to give Aja-kala the wife of Udana as a pledge.

129. TCS 1 158 (TCS 1 pl. 7)

1. na-ba-sa$_6$
2. ù-na-a-dug$_4$
3. géme lú-^{d}dumu-zi-ke$_4$ in-tuk-a
4. [zí]d-KA-šè
5. na-ba-dù
6. géme du$_{11}$-ga-ni-zi-kam

Tell Nabasa not to detain the servant girl that Lu-Dumuzi has married, because of the KA-flour. She is a servant girl of Duganizi!

130. TCS 1 159 (ITT 3 5058)

1. na-ba-sa_6-ra
2. ù-na-a-dug_4
3. dam da-da-ra
4. zíd pad-ra-šè
5. úgu-a-na nu-ub-gál
6. na-ba-dù

Tell Nabasa not to detain the wife of Dada (just because) there are no flour subsistence (rations) on his account!

131. TCS 1 229 (BM 25410)

1. ur-^{d}lama
2. ù-na-a-dug_4
3. dam lugal-a-ru-a-ka
4. a-šà-ga-ni
5. ^{d}amar-^{d}sìn-ur-sag-e
6. ba-ab-gub
7. a-šà in-dab_5-ba-na
8. na-ba-a-dù

Tell Ur-Lama that Amar-Sin-ursag has occupied the field of the wife (i.e. probably "widow") of Lugal-arua. He cannot retain the field that he has seized!

132. NBC 9268

1. nu-úr-^{d}sìn
2. ù-na-a-dug_4
3. dam ur-^{d}da-mu šitim
4. šu ḫa-ba-re

Seal: ur-gá šitim gal
^{d}en-líl-lá
lú-^{d}nanna
dub-sar
dumu-ni

Tell Nur-Sin to release the wife of Ur-Damu, the mason.

Seal: O Urga, master mason of (the god) Enlil—Lu-Nanna, scribe, is his son!

Personnel Matters

133. TCS 1 32 (BM 134633)

1. ⸢a⸣-tá-na-aḫ
2. ù-na-a-dug$_4$
3. gìr-sè-ga lú-bi-ka
4. má-a ù-mi-ú
5. gìri-ni-mu
6. ḫa-mu-na-ab-šúm-mu
7. e$_4$-ma-ru-kam
8. ul$_4$-la-bi
9. ḫé-ma-gub

Tell Atanah to give to Girinemu Lubi's domestics after they have arrived by boat—it is urgent, he is to do it quickly—(tell) him to be at my service!

134. BM 18568

1. lú-^{d}nin-gír-su-ra
2. ù-na-a-dug$_4$
3. ^{d}ig-alim-ì-sa$_6$-ra
4. 1 túg ḫé-na-ab-šúm-mu
5. im še-ba síg-ba
6. ga-bí-gi

Seal: ba-zi
dub-sar
dumu šeš-šeš

Tell Lu-Ningirsu to give a garment to Igalim-isa (and) that I will confirm (it on) the (account) tablet of the grain and garment rations.

Seal: Bazi, scribe, son of Sheshshesh.

135. TCS 1 39 (U 3414)

1. a-kal-la
2. ù-na-a-dug$_4$
3. su-ú-na-a lú-mu-ra
4. inim-ma-ni di ḫé-bé
5. tukum-bi
6. lú di-da-ka-ni
7. giš la-ba-ra-an-ur$_4$
8. ká é-gal-šè
9. mu lugal pàd-mu-ni-ib

Tell Aja-kala to hear the legal complaint of my man Su'una. If his litigant does not abandon all claims against him, make him swear by the name of the king at the gate of the palace.

136. TCS 1 47 (UIOM 491)

1. ba-za
2. ù-na-a-dug$_4$
3. 1 ad-KID
4. ud 1-šè
5. ḫa-mu-na-šúm-mu

Seal: lú-kal-la
dub-sar

Tell Baza to give him a basket-weaver for a day.

Seal: Lu-kala, scribe.

137. Gelinas, 1965:63.

1. ba-na-na
2. ù-na-a-dug$_4$
3. 3.3.5 še gur
4. še-ba tur-tur-ne
5. ḫé-na-ab-šúm-mu

Reverse unavailable

Tell Banana to give him 1,130 liters of grain as rations for the youngsters.

138. BM 12492

1. lú-^{d}utu
2. ù ur-^{d}nanše-ra
3. ù-ne-a-dug$_4$
4. ^{I}ur-^{d}lama
5. ^{I}lú-^{d}nin-dar-a
6. ^{I}lú-ka-gi-na
7. ^{I}ḫé-sa$_6$-mu
8. zíd-KA nu-àr-re
9. šu ḫa-bar-re

Tell Lu-Utu and Ur-Nanshe to release Ur-Lama, Lu-Nindara, Lu-kagina, (and) Hesamu, who have not ground the KA-flour.

139. TU 225

1. 0.5.0.0 še (gur) ur-sukkal
2. 0.5.0.0 še (gur) šeš-kal-la
3. 0.5.0.0 še (gur) sag-^{d}nanna
4. 0.5.0.0 še (gur) lú-^{d}[b]a-Ú
5. 0.5.0.0 še (gur) ur-^{d}a-zi-mú-a
6. 0.5.0.0 še (gur) ur-^{d}ba-Ú
7. 0.5.0.0 še (gur) ur-mes
8. 0.5.0.0 še (gur) lú-^{d}inanna
9. 0.5.0.0 še (gur) ur-gar
10. 0.5.0.0 še (gur) ⌜lugal⌝-^{giš}gigir-re
11. 2.0.0.0 gur
12. má-[l]aḫ$_5$ má lugal-šè DU-me
13. iti amar-a-a-si
14. ur-^{giš}gigir-ra ù-⌜na-a-dug$_4$⌝ ḫa-ma-ab-[šúm]-mu
15. mu má-gur$_8$ maḫ ba-dím

Seal: lú- . . . dub-sar

Sixty liters of grain for Ur-sukkal, 60 liters of grain for Shesh-kala, 60 liters of grain for Sag-Nanna, 60 liters of grain for Lu-Ba'u, 60 liters of grain for Ur-Azimua, 60 liters of grain for Ur-Ba'u, 60 liters of grain for Ur-mes, 60 liters of grain for Lu-Inanna, 60 liters of grain for Ur-gar, (and) 60 for Lugal-gigir. (In total) 600 liters (of grain as rations for) the sailors posted to the royal barge. Month of Amar-Ajasi (Girsu month ten). Tell Ur-gigir to give (the grain) to them.

The year that the mighty barge was built (= Shu-Sin year 8).

Seal: Lu-. . . , scribe.

140. Owen, *Or*NS 40:388

1. [. . .]-KA [x]x-ra
2. ù-na-dug$_4$
3. 2 guruš mu-gi$_4$
4. 2 u$_4$-àm
5. ḫé-na-ab-zi-zi

Tell [so-and-so] to debit to him (the wages) of two returned workers for two days.

141. TCS 1 81 (RIAA 198 = TSU 7)

1. èr-ra
2. ù-na-a-dug$_4$
3. ab-ba-kal-la
4. ur-mes-ra
5. zi lugal
6. gá-e-me
7. ḫa-na-šúm

Seal: géme-^{d}lama
nin-dingir ^{d}nanše
igi-^{d}inanna-šè
dub-sar
árad-zu

Tell Era that I swear by the life of the king, it was I who gave Abba-kala to Ur-mes.

Seal: O Geme-Lama, high priestess of (the goddess) Nanshe, Igi-Inannashe, scribe, is your servant!

142. TCS 1 95 (UET 3 7)

1. [l]ú-du$_{10}$-ga
2. ù-na-a-dug$_{4}$
3. 10 érin é-lugal-la^{ki}
4. 20 érin ga-eš$_{5}$^{ki}
5. kaskal-šè-àm
6. ḫé-em-gi$_{4}$-gi$_{4}$
7. ^{kuš}a-gá-lá è-[a?]
8. é-e [. . . ḫ]é-[ne-éb-šúm-mu]
9. e$_{4}$-ma-ru-kam
10. u[l$_{4}$-l]a-bi

Tell Lu-duga to send me ten conscripts from (the hamlet of) Elugala and 20 conscripts from (the town of) Gaesh; they are (to go on) an expedition. [*Have them equipped with*] packs (for provisions). It is urgent! (Do it) quickly!

143. Owen, *Or*NS 40:394

1. ur-^{d}nanna-ka
2. ù-na-a-dug$_{4}$
3. ⌜á⌝ guruš u$_{4}$ 5-kam
4. [ḫé-n]a-ab-šúm-⌜mu⌝

Rest destroyed

Tell Ur-Nanna to provide wages for the workers for five days . . .

144. TCS 1 110 (ITT 3 5558)

1. lú-kal-la-ra
2. ù-na-a-dug$_{4}$
3. lú še-ba àga-uš lugal-ka ba-an-si-ga
4. mu-didli-šè
5. síg-ba-bi
6. ḫa-ba-ab-šúm-mu
7. [i]m síg-ba ba-[gá-g]á èn ḫa-ab-tar-re

Tell Lu-kala to give the wool rations to those who get grain rations and have been made royal constables. (Tell) him to make certain that each individual is entered on the wool ration (account) tablet(s).

145. TCS 1 212 (ITT 4 8150)

1. ur-^{d}ba-Ú
2. ù-na-a-dug$_4$
3. 45 má-laḫ$_4$ še 0.0.5-ta
4. 90 šu-ku$_6$ 11? [lú] má gal-gal-[la]
5. 130 guruš [x] dumu dab$_5$-ba
6. ugula ša-ar-[ì]-lí
7. gìri má še-giš-ì-ka

Tell Ur-Ba'u: 45 sailors (with pay) of 50 liters (of grain) each, 90 fishermen, *11* large-boat sailors, 130 workers, [x] pressed men (all) under the supervision of Shar-ili. (A crew) for the journey of the boat with (a cargo) of sesame.

146. TCS 1 216 (TCS 1 pl. 12)

1. ur-gi$_6$-par$_4$
2. ù-na-a-dug$_4$
3. guruš 10-àm
4. má dug ba-al-e-dè
5. lú-^{d}šára-ra
6. ḫé-na-šúm-mu
7. lú-ús-[s]á ḫé-eb-da-an-gi$_4$-gi$_4$

Tell Ur-gipar to give Lu-Shara workmen—ten of them—for unloading a boat(load) of pots (and) to send (some) *escorts.*

147. TCS 1 227 (BM 25828)

1. ur-kisal-ra
2. ù-na-a-dug$_4$
3. ur-bàd-bi$_7$-ra
4. ud 30-àm
5. lú-^{d}iškur-ra
6. ḫé-na-šúm-mu

Tell Ur-kisal to give Ur-Badbira to Lu-Ishkur for 30 days.

148. TCS 1 290 (TCS 1 pl. 16)

1. šà-nin-gá-ra
2. ù-na-a-dug$_4$
3. im érin diri a-pi$_4$-šal$_4$^{ki} ù gú-eden-na

4. pisan-gá ù-mu-ni-gá-ar
5. ur-ama-na-ra
6. ḫa-mu-na-ab-šúm-mu
7. e$_4$-ma-ru-kam
8. na-mu-nigin

Tell Shaninga to give Ur-amana the (account) tablets concerning the additional conscripts for (the city of) Apishal (and the) Guedena (borderland) after he has placed them in my (account) basket. It is urgent! (Tell) him not to *keep it!*

149. TCS 1 298 (Gomi—Sato 191)

1. šeš-kal-⌜la-ra?⌝
2. ù-na-a-dug$_4$
3. ì-ba ḫé-⌜dab$_5$⌝
4. é ba-gára ù
5. é gá-tùm-dùg
6. nam-maḫ-ra
7. ḫa-na-⌜ab⌝-šúm-mu
8. mu si-mu-ur-ru-um^{ki} ba-⌜ḫul⌝

Illegible seal

Tell Shesh-kala to give Nammah the oil rations for the hedab-workers of the Bagara temple estate and the temple estate of (the goddess) Gatumdug.

Year Simurum was defeated (= Ibbi-Sin year 3).

150. TCS 1 325 (ITT 5 6969)

1. x-x-ra
2. ù-na-a-dug$_4$
3. 30 adda udu
4. ^{giš}tukul-e dab$_5$-ba
5. gu$_7$-dè
6. ur-^{d}al-la-ra
7. ḫé-na-ab-šúm-mu

Seal: ur-[mes]
dub-[sar]
dumu gù-[dé-a]

Tell . . . to give Ur-Alla 30 sheep carcasses for consumption by the prisoners of war.

Seal: Ur-mes, scribe, son of Gudea.

151. TCS 1 128 (ITT 3 6155)

1. lú-^{d}šára
2. ù-na-a-dug$_4$
3. 1 ur-^{d}lama
4. ù ba-za
5. lú na-an-ba-dù
6. zé-e-me maškim-a-ni
7. ḫ[é]-me

Tell Lu-Shara that no one should detain Ur-Lama and Baza. You yourself should serve as their (lit., his) bailiff.

Financial Affairs

152. TCS 1 131 (TCS 1 pl. 6)

1. ⌜lú-^{d}šára⌝-[ra$^?$]
2. ù-na-a-dug$_4$
3. 1 gín kù-babbar-àm
4. mu-mu-šè
5. ba-sa$_6$-ga
6. ḫé-na-ab-šúm-mu
7. na-mi-gur-re
8. a-ba šeš-mu-gin$_7$
9. kù-bi ud 4-kam-ka
10. lú kin-gi$_4$-a-mu
11. ra-an-túm
12. šeš-mu me ša di-mu

Tell Lu-Shara to give one shekel of silver to Basaga on my behalf. (The matter) must not come up again! Who is (as good) as my brother? My messenger will bring that silver to you in four days. My brother . . . .

153. TCS 1 370 (TCS 1 pl. 21)
(Akkadian)

1. *um-ma* šu-ku-ku
2. *a-na* an-da-ga
3. *qí-bí-ma*
4. 3 MA.NA KÙ.BABBAR
5. KI DUMU DAM.GÀR GI.NÉ
6. *šu-bi-lam*
7. *mi-nu-um aš-tá-na-pá-ra-ma*
8. *la tù-ša-ba-lam*

Thus says Shu-Kuku: Tell Andaga: Send me three minas of silver, guaranteed by an *assistant* commercial agent (or: with a trustworthy commercial agent)! Why do I have to write to you time and time again and you never send (the money) to me?

154. TCS 1 268 (Ni 1501)

1. ur-sukkal
2. ù-na-dug$_4$
3. ḫa-la-mu
4. úgu-mu
5. níg-na-me
6. nu-ub-tuku

Tell Ur-sukkal that I owe nothing to Halamu.

155. Foster, *ASJ* 12:54
(Akkadian)

1. *a-na* dingir-sa$_6$-ga
2. *qí-bí-ma*
3. 1 GÍN KÙ.BABBAR
4. *a-na* ur-^{d}šul-pa-è
5. *li-dì-in*
6. EGIR BURU$_{14}$.ŠÈ
7. 1.2.0.0 ŠE GUR
8. ⌜ŠÚM.MU⌝. DAM
9. *a-wa-tum*
10. *la ì-tu-ra-am*

Seal: šu-^{d}šul-g[i]
aga-uš lugal
dumu i-la-a

Tell Dingir-saga to give Ur-Shulpae one shekel of silver. He is to repay 420 liters of barley after the harvest. The matter must not come up again!

Seal: Shu-Shulgi, royal constable, son of Ilaja.

156. TCS 1 269 (TCS 1 pl. 15)

1. ur-^{d}šára
2. ù-na-a-dug$_4$
3. 1/2 gín kù-babbar
4. é-zi-mu
5. ḫa-na-ab-šúm-mu
6. gá-e ù-gin
7. ga-na-ab-šúm

Tell Ur-Shara to give Ezimu half a shekel of silver. (Tell) him that I myself will give it (back) to him when I arrive.

157. MVN 3 350

1. lú-^{d}sìn
2. ù dingir-sa$_{6}$-ga
3. ù-na-a-dug$_{4}$
4. 3 gín kù-sig$_{17}$ ḫuš
5. 9 gín kù-babbar
6. da-a-a
7. ḫé-na-ab-šúm-mu

Tell Lu-Su'ena and Dingir-saga to give Daja three shekels of red gold and nine shekels of silver.

Agricultural Matters

158. MVN 6 429 = ITT 4 7450

1. lugal-gú-gal-ra
2. ù-na-a-dug$_{4}$
3. 22 gún gi zi
4. dingir-sukkal-ra
5. ḫé-na-ab-šúm-mu
6. na-mi-gur-re
7. e$_{4}$-ma-ru-kam
8. a-ba šeš-mu-ke$_{4}$

Tell Lugal-gugal to give Dingir-sukkal 22 talents of *young* reeds. (The matter) must not come up again! It is urgent! Who is (as good) as my brother?

159. MVN 4 179

1. 1.0.0 (gur) še ba zag-mu
2. ba-zi-zi lunga
3. ḫé-na-ab-šúm-mu
4. iti ezen-^{d}šul-gi
5. mu ^{d}amar-^{d}sìn lugal
   ur-bí-lum mu-ḫul

Seal: árad-mu
dub-sar
dumu ur-⸢nigar^{gar}⸣ kuš$_{7}$

Tell him to give the brewer Bazizi 300 liters of grain as rations for the New Year (festival).

Month of the Festival of Shulgi (= Umma month 10). The year that the king Amar-Sin defeated Urbilum (Amar-Sin year 2).

Seal: Arad-mu, scribe, son of Ur-nigar, the equerry.

160. BM 15497

1. lú-má-gu-la
2. ù-na-a-dug$_4$
3. 5 sìla ninda
4. ur-^{d}nin-líl
5. ḫé-na-ab-šúm-mu
6. kišib ^{d}šul-gi-kù-zu

Seal: ^{d}šul-gi-kù-zu
dub-sar
dumu [^{d}šára . . .]
[dub-sar]

Tell Lu-magula to give Ur-Ninlil five liters of bread. Seal of Shulgi-kuzu.

Seal: Shulgi-kuzu, scribe, son of Shara-. . . , [scribe]

161. TCS 1 174 (BM 25835)

1. na-ni
2. ù-na-dug$_4$
3. 5.0.0 še gur lugal
4. še ur$_5$ -ra
5. lugal-me-lám dumu ur-ma-ma
6. in-na-šúm-ma
7. lú na-ba-dù

Tell Nani that no one is to hold back the 1500 royal liters of grain—grain (meant as) an interest bearing loan—that I have given to Lugal-melam, son of Ur-Mama.

162. TCS 1 33 (YOS 4 140)

1. a-tu-ra
2. ù-na-a-dug$_4$
3. a-šà a-na an-uru$_4$-a
4. maš 1 1/2 gín-ta
5. ḫé-ša-lá-e
6. lú-^{d}šára-ke$_4$

Tell Atu to pay Lu-Shara a rent of one and one half shekel of silver (per iku) for whatever (part of) the field he will till.

163. TCS 1 49 (BM 25205)

1. ba-zi
2. ù-na-a-dug_4
3. gaba a-šà ^{d}nin-á
4. a-šà lú lunga-ke_4-ne-ka
5. á-bi-a
6. a-šà 3 (bùr) GÁNA
7. ì-gál-la
8. lugal-uru-da a-šà-mu bí-dug_4
9. ḫa-ba-da-kar-re
10. lú-dingir-ra
11. ḫé-na-ab-šúm-mu
12. nam-mi-gur-re

Bordering on the field of (the god/goddess) Nin'a, within the field of the brewers, along its side, there is a field (measuring) three bur. Lugal-uruda said, "It is my field." Tell Bazi to take it away (from Lugal-uruda), and to give it to Lu-dingira. (The matter) must not come up again!

164. TCS 1 53 (Gomi—Sato 44)

Tablet:

1. da-da-mu
2. ù-na-a-dug_4
3. 12.0.0 še gur lugal
4. ur-$^{d}si_4$-an-na
5. ma-an-bal
6. ḫé-na-ab-zi-zi

Envelope:

1. da-da-mu
2. ù-na-a-dug_4
3. 12.0.0 še gur lugal
4. ur-$^{d}si_4$-an-na-ke_4
5. ma-an-bal
6. ḫé-⌜na⌝-ab-zi-zi
7. kišib ur-^{d}nin-giz-zi-da dumu lugal-sa_6-ga
8. mu ús-sa ki-maš^{ki} ba-ḫul

Seal: ur-^{d}nin-giz-zi-da
dumu
lugal-sa_6-ga

Tablet:

Tell Dadamu to issue the 3,600 liters of grain which Ur-Si'ana has turned over to me.

Envelope:

Tell Dadamu to issue the 3,600 liters of grain which Ur-Si'ana has turned over to me.

Seal of Ur-Ningizida, son of Lugal-saga.

The year after (the year) Kimash was sacked (= Shulgi year 48).

Seal: Ur-Ningizida, scribe, son of Lugal-saga.

165. TCS 1 66 (BM 25822)

1. gù-dé-a
2. ù-na-a-dug4
3. a-šà ur-^{d}šul-pa-è
4. ur-^{d}ig-alim-ra
5. di-bi nu-ì-dab$_5$
6. še-bi ur-^{d}šul-pa-è-ka
7. la-ba-ku$_4$
8. še-ba šu ḫé-na-bar-re

Tell Gudea that as far as the field of Ur-Shulpae is concerned, the judgment did not go in favor of Ur-Igalim. Its grain has not been delivered to Ur-Shulpae; (tell) him (Gudea) to release that grain!

166. YOS 15 99

1. lú-^{d}šul-⌜gi⌝-ra
2. ù-na-a-dug$_4$
3. a-šà-mu
4. uru$_4$-lá-šè
5. ì-kal-la
6. ⌜in-na⌝-x[. . .]
7. lú nam-ba-[. . .]
8. a-ba šeš-mu-gin$_7$

Tell Lu-Shulgi that no one is to . . . my field which he had . . . to Ikala for cultivation. Who is (as good) as my brother?

167. MVN 15 366

1. ba-a-lum
2. ù-na-a-dug$_4$
3. 6.0.0 še gur
4. mu zì-da-šè
5. i-pí-iq-na-ni
6. ḫé-na-ab-šúm-⌜mu⌝
7. ⌜na⌝-mi-gur-re
8. dub-ba-ni ⌜šu⌝ ḫa-ba-ti-ti

Tell Ba'alum to give Ipiq-Nani 1,800 liters of grain for (making) flour. (The matter) must not come up again! (Tell him) to take his receipt!

168. TCS 1 246 (Owen, *OrNS* 40:396)

1. ur-nigar⌜gar⌝-ra
2. ù-na-a-dug$_4$
3. 5.0.0 še gur
4. 0.1.0 dabin
5. 0.3.0 dida gin
6. 0.1.0 eša
7. dingir-mu-da-dah-ra
8. ḫé-na-ab-šúm-mu

Tell Ur-nigar to give Dingir-mudadah 1,500 liters of grain, 60 liters of dabin flour, 180 liters of ordinary beer (and) 60 liters of esha flour.

169. TCS 1 78 (BM 21522)

1. igi-an-na-ke$_4$-zu-⌜ra?⌝
2. ù-na-a-dug$_4$
3. še-àm
4. 1.0.0 gur
5. nin-dingir ^{d}gá-tùm-dùg
6. ḫa-na-ab-šúm-mu
7. na-mi-gur-re

Tell Igi-Anakezu to give the grain in question—300 liters—to the high priestess of (the goddess) Gatumdug. (The matter) must not come up again!

170. TCS 1 80 (YOS 4 115)

1. èr-⌜ra⌝
2. ù-na-a-du[g$_4$]
3. ^{giš}kiri$_6$ da-⌜a⌝-da-mu
4. inim-mu-ta
5. [ḫ]é-eb-sa$_{10}$-sa$_{10}$
6. lú-na-me inim nu-un-gá-gá
7. [t]ukum-bi ⌜lú⌝-na-me inim ⌜bí-in⌝-[gar]
8. gú-[. . .] lú ki i[nim-ma-b]i-me-è[n]

Tell Era to purchase the orchard of Da'adamu on my responsibility (lit., by my order). No one should raise a claim against it. If someone does raise a claim . . . you will be the witness (in the matter).

171. TCS 1 92 (Gomi—Sato 224)

1. lú-bi-mu-ra
2. ù-na-a-dug$_4$
3. nam-maḫ-ra
4. 1.0.0 še gur lugal in-na-an-šúm-ma-aš
5. nam-ba-an-dù
6. ⌜lugal!⌝ á zi-ga-na
7. šu ḫé-ba-re

Tell Lubimu that since he has paid 300 royal liters of grain for Nammah, he should not be detained. (Tell) him that *the person who wronged him* must release him!

172. TCS 1 102 (UDT 33)

1. lú-gu-la-mu
2. ù-na-a-dug$_4$
3. ì-kal-la
4. še na-šid šu ba-bi bí-dug$_4$
5. 20.0.0 gur-ba
6. šu ḫé-bar-re
7. gá-e ki níg-ŠID-ka ga-[na-ab-z]i
8. é-[kišib]-ba-ka
9. ga-na-ab-zi
10. egir$_5$-ni-ta ŠID-gá ma-a-dug$_4$
11. šu ḫé-bar-re
12. na-mi-gur-re

Tell Lu-gula: Ikala said: "The grain has been tallied: release it!" (Tell him [Lu-gula]) to release 6,000 liters from this (amount)! I myself will issue it at the accounting office, or I will issue it from the storehouse. He promised me that afterwards (or after his death) it would be in my account. (Tell him) to release it. (The matter) must not come up again!

173. TCS 1 109 (Fish, *MCS* 3:2)

1. lú-kal-la
2. ù-na-a-dug$_4$
3. 2.0.0 še gur lugal
4. ur-^{d}ḫendur-sag lunga
5. 0.2.0 še numun 0.1.0 še-ba-a-ni
6. ì-lí-bí-la-ni
7. 0.1.0 za-ri-iq
8. 0.1.0 ur-^{d}sumukan
9. a-šà-ta lag ri-ri-[ga]-dè
10. ḫé-ne-eb-šúm-mu
11. mu lugal ḫé-a-pàd
12. 1 sìla še kù 1 še$^{!}$(sìla)-gin$_7$
13. igi-zu-nu-bad ba-gi$_4$-gi$_4$
14. á-ág-gá a-šà-ga
15. a-na bí-du$_{11}$-ga
16. šu ḫé-eb-du$_7$
17. má-mu ^{d}utu-ì-‹lí› in-ku$_4$-ku$_4$-da
18. ud nu-mu-zal-e
19. níg a-na bí-du$_{11}$-ga ḫé-eb-gá-gá

Tell Lu-kala to give 600 liters of grain to Ur-Hendursaga, the brewer, 120 liters of seed grain, and 60 liters of grain as his ration to Ili-bilanni, 60 liters to Zariq, (and) 60 liters to Ur-Sumukan, (as payment) for removing clods from the field.

(Tell him) to take an oath on the king's name that Igizu-nubad has been reimbursed *(at the rate of) one barleycorn of silver for one liter of grain.*

(Tell) him to complete the field work (that I) ordered, to the extent that he promised!

(Tell him), before (even) a day passes, to place (all the) things I have ordered in the boat that Shamash-ili will bring!

174. TCS 1 112 (ITT 5 6900)

1. lú-nam-tar-ra
2. ù-na-a-dug$_4$
3. 0.3.0 še
4. a-kal-la
5. ḫé-an-ši-dab$_5$
6. en-na énsi-ra
7. ì-na-ab-bé
8. dub-ba-ni
9. ḫé-ma-an-tùm

Tell Lu-namtar that Aja-kala is to take possession of 180 liters of grain. (Let him know) that until he has spoken to the city governor, he must bring me his tablet.

175. TCS 1 124 (NATN 807)

1. lú-sa$_6$-g[a]
2. ù-na-a-dug$_4$
3. ùr-re-ba-ab-du$_7$
4. ù nu-úr-^{d}IŠKUR
5. é-e gál ḫa-ab-tag$_4$-tag$_4$
6. še níg-gù-dé-a-ni-gin$_7$
7. šu ḫa-ba-ab-ti-ti
8. na-mi-gur-re
9. e$_4$-ma-ru-kam

Seal: ^{d}i-bí-^{d}sìn
lugal kala-ga
lugal uri$_5$^{ki}-ma
lugal an ub-da límmu-ba
a-ḫu-ba-[ni]
dub-sar
‹árad-zu›

Tell Lu-saga to open the house for Ure-babdu and Nur-Adad and to have them take as much grain as he demands. (The matter) must not come up again! It is urgent!

Seal: O Ibbi-Sin, mighty king, king of Ur, king of the four corners of the universe, Ahu-bani, scribe ‹is your servant› !

176. TCS 1 125 (TCS 1 pl. 5)

1. lú-sa$_6$-ga-ra
2. ù-na-a-dug$_4$
3. a-na-áš-àm
4. puzur$_4$-ha-ià

5. mu še kur-ra-šè
6. še eštub ḫ̮é-na-šúm
7. lú-ni á ba-an-zi
8. en-na àm-gin
9. igi-mu-šè inim-bi a-bal-e
10. na-ba-an-dù

Seal: ^{d}i-bí-^{d}sìn
lugal kala-ga
lugal uri$_{5}^{ki}$-ma
lugal an ub-da límmu-ba
ur-^{d}šu-maḫ̮
dub-sar
dumu ur-nigar^{gar}
árad-zu

Ask Lu-saga why he gave Puzur-Haja "carp" grain instead of "mountain" grain. His man has done wrong. (Tell him) that until I arrive, (and) he discusses the matter with me, he is not to be detained.

Seal: O Ibbi-Sin, mighty king, king of Ur, king of the four corners of the universe, Ur-Shumah, scribe, the son of Ur-nigar, is your servant!

177. TCS 1 153 (BM 85497)

1. lugal-iti-da-ra
2. ù-na-a-dug$_4$
3. a-šà na-kab$_x$(DA)-tum
4. nim ù lú kar-ḫ̮ar^{ki}-ra-ke$_4$-ne
5. šúm-mu-da
6. ⌜in⌝-na-a-du$_{11}$-ga
7. ḫ̮é-ne-eb-šúm-mu
8. ù 6 (bùr) GÁNA
9. tu-tá-ru-um-ra
10. ḫ̮é-na-ab-šúm-mu

Tell Lugal-itida to give the Elamites and men of Karahar the Nakkabtum field which he/I had promised to give them. Furthermore: (Tell him) to give six bur of land to Tutarum.

178. BM 18583

1. ur-^{d}ba-Ú
2. ù-na-a-dug$_4$
3. 60.0.0 še gur lugal
4. lá-u$_x$(NI) ur-^{d}nanše dumu lú-du$_{10}$-ga
5. úgu-mu-a
6. ḫ̮a-gá-gá
7. bar-mu-šè šu ḫ̮e-ba-re

Tell Ur-Ba'u to put 18,000 liters of grain, the arrears of Ur-Nanshe, son of Lu-duga, on my account. (Tell) him to release it on my responsibility.

179. BM 18903

1. lú-^{d}nin-šubur-ra
2. ù-na-a-dug$_4$
3. 12.0.0 še gur
4. še níg-gál-la-a
5. ka$_5$^{a}-mu
6. in-na-sar-a-ra
7. en-na u$_4$-sakar-šè
8. ḫé-ši-dab$_5$

Tell Lu-Ninshubur that as concerns the 3,600 liters of grain, stocks of Kajamu, which are written down (on) his (account), he must take possession (of them) before the new moon!

180. BM 20174

1. ḫa-bù-bù
2. ù-na-a-dug$_4$
3. 0.0.1 zíz
4. lú-^{d}iškur
5. ḫa-mu-na-ab-šúm-mu
6. dub-ba-ni-ta
7. ga-ab-ta-tur

Tell Habubu to give ten liters of emmer wheat to Lu-Ishkur (and) that I will deduct it from his (account)-tablet.

181. BM 21684

1. šà-kù-ge-ra
2. ù-na-a-dug$_4$
3. 0.0.3 še lugal
4. ur-gar-ra
5. ḫé-na-ab-šúm-mu
6. na-mi-gur-re
7. dub-ba-ni šu na-ba-ši-íb-ti

Seal: ur-^{d}ba-ú
dub-sar
dumu lú-du$_{10}$-ga
sanga ^{d}nin-gír-su

Tell Shakuge to give 30 liters of grain to Ur-gar. (The matter) must not come up again! He is not to receive his tablet.

Seal: Ur-Ba'u, scribe, son of Lu-duga, the chief temple administrator of (the god) Ningirsu.

182. BM 22042

1. ur-^{d}ḫendur-sag-ka-ke$_4$
2. na-ab-bé-a
3. ur-^{d}ba-Ú
4. ù-na-a-dug$_4$
5. 60.0.0 še gur
6. á gud
7. ì-du$_8$
8. bur-^{d}IŠKUR-ra
9. ḫé-ab-šúm-mu

Thus says Ur-Hendursaga: Tell Ur-Ba'u to give 18,000 liters of grain, the hire for oxen, to the doorkeeper of Bur-Adad.

183. TCS 1 288 (MVN 7 51 = ITT 4 7651)

1. šabra-ra
2. ù-⸢na-dug$_4$⸣
3. 10.0.0 še gur lugal
4. lú-^{d}nanše-ra
5. ḫé-na-ab-zi-zi
6. úgu šeš-mu dam-gàr-ka
7. ḫé-gá-gá

Tell the prefect to issue 3,000 liters of grain to Lu-Nanshe. (Tell) him to put it on the account of the merchant Sheshmu.

184. TENUS 482 = MVN 15 218

1. lú-^{d}šul-gi-ra
2. ù-na-dug$_4$
3. 1 udu ur-^{d}iškur ì-dab$_5$
4. ur-^{d}ḫendur-sag-gá
5. še-na šu ḫa-mu-na-a-ba-re

Tell Lu-Shulgi that Ur-Ishkur has received a sheep (and) that Ur-Hendursaga is to release (feed) grain for him.

185. Lafont, *RA* 84:169 no. 3

1. ab-ba-kal-la
2. ù-⸢na-a-dug$_4$⸣
3. zíd-⸢KA en?⸣-te
4. ur-⸢mes⸣ šabra-šè
5. lú-nam-tar-ra
6. na-ba-dù
7. pisan-dub-ba ga-na-zi

Tell Abba-kala not to detain Lu-namtar (just) because of the winter KA-flour of Ur-mes, the prefect. I will issue it myself from the central accounts (lit., tablet-basket).

186. Lafont, *RA* 84:169 no. 1

1. lú-^{d}nin-šu[bur-ra]
2. ù-na-a-dug$_{4}$
3. še a-šà du$_{6}$-ḫi-li-ba
4. šu ì-íb-ba
5. na-ba-a-dù

Rest broken

Tell Lu-Ninshubur not to retain the released grain from the Duhiliba field . . . .

187. MVN 15 368

1. en-nu-um-ì-lí
2. ù-na-a-dug$_{4}$
3. 1.0.0 še gur
4. ḫu-la-ni
5. ḫé-na-ab-šúm-mu

Seal: ^{d}šu-^{d}sin
lugal kala-ga
lugal uri$_{5}^{ki}$-ma
lugal an-ub-da límmu-ba
lú-^{d}[. . .]
dub-[sar]
dumu [. . .]
árad-[zu]

Tell Ennum-ili to give Hulani 300 liters of grain.

Seal: O Shu-Sin, mighty king, king of Ur, king of the four quarters of the universe, Lu-[x], scribe, son of [x], is your servant!

188. MVN 3 226

1. lú-gi-na
2. ù-na-dug$_{4}$
3. 60.0.0 še gur še numun-ta
4. mu ur-nigar sag apin-šè
5. lú-^{d}šára dumu ur-^{giš}gigir-ra-ka
6. ḫé-na-ab-šúm-mu
7. ḫé-sa$_{6}$ dub-sar maškim
8. a-šà sum$_{4}$-ma-ra
9. iti ^{d}li$_{9}$-si$_{4}$
10. mu ^{d}amar-^{d}sìn
11. lugal-e ur-bí-lum mu-ḫul

Seal: árad-⌜mu⌝
dub-sar
dumu ur-nigar^{gar}

Tell Lu-gina to give Lu-Shara, the son of Ur-gigir, 18,000 liters of grain from the seed grain (stocks) for Ur-nigar, the head plowman. Hesa, the scribe, (is to be) the conveyor.

(For) the Sumara field.

Month of the (goddess) Lisi (= Umma month 3). The year (king) Amar-Sin destroyed Urbilum (= Amar-Sin year 2).

Seal: Arad-mu, scribe, son of Ur-nigar.

189. NBC 8861

1. šu-^{d}ba-Ú
2. ù-na-a-dug$_4$
3. 3.0.0 še gur
4. ^{d}šára-kam-e
5. šà-gal-la-ni-šè
6. é ^{d}šu-^{d}sìn-šè
7. ḫa-ab-ta-ab-è-e

Tell Shu-Ba'u to issue 900 liters of grain to Sharakam for his food for/from the temple household of (king) Shu-Sin.

190. TCS 1 311 (UET 3 2)

1. šu-^{d}nin-šubur
2. ù-na-a-dug$_4$
3. a-šà ki gud 2-kam
4. gud apin
5. ù engar š[à?-gu]d?
6. ⌜ḫé⌝-bi-[ib]-sì-ge
7. ù 70.0.0 še gur-àm
8. zag 10 ^{d}nin-gal-ke$_4$
9. ḫa-ba-ab-šúm-mu
10. gaba-ri dub pisan-dub-ba
11. iti ezen-maḫ
12. mu en ^{d}inanna máš-e ì-p[àd]

Tell Shu-Ninshubur to assign plow oxen and ox-drivers for a field (usually) plowed by two oxen (and) to give 21,000 liters of grain as the tithe to (the temple of the goddess) Ningal. (This) is a copy of the chief accountant's tablet.

Month of the Great Festival (= Ur month 10). The year that the main priest of (the goddess) Inanna was chosen by omen (= Ibbi-Sin year 10).

191. TCS 1 299 (YOS 4 121)

1. [šeš]-kal-la-ra
2. ù-na-a-dug$_4$
3. 0.2.2.4 sìla še ‹gur› lugal
4. níg-dab$_5$ en-en-e-ne
5. níg-sa$_6$-ga-ar
6. ḫé-na-ab-šúm-mu
7. ezen-^{d}dumu-zi

Tell Shesh-kala to give Nigsaga 144 liters of grain as offering(s) to the (shades of the dead) rulers.

(For) the Festival of Dumuzi.

192. TCS 1 305 (YOS 4 134)

1. šeš-kal-la
2. ù-na-a-dug$_4$
3. 0.1.3 lú-eb-gal
4. 0.1.3 lú-^{d}šára
5. še pad-e tag$_4$-a
6. ḫé-na-ab-šúm-mu
7. mu kišib nu-ub-⌜ra⌝-šè
8. na-mi-íb-gur-e

Tell Shesh-kala to give 90 liters (of grain) to Lu-Ebgal (and) 90 liters to Lu-Shara—grain that is left over for subsistence (rations). (The matter) must not come up again (just) because no seal has been rolled (on this document)!

193. TCS 1 306 (YOS 4 118)

1. šeš-kal-la
2. ù-na-a-dug$_4$
3. lú-^{d}nanna-ra
4. en$_8$ ù-na-tar
5. še-ba ur-lugal
6. guru$_7$-a a-na mu-un-tag$_4$-a
7. ḫa-mu-na-ab-šúm-mu

Tell Shesh-kala to give him (i.e., the bearer of this tablet) the grain rations of Ur-lugal, as much as is left over in the granary, after having checked the matter with Lu-Nanna.

194. TCS 1 307 (YOS 4 119)

1. šeš-kal-la
2. ù lú-^{d}nan[na-r]a
3. ù-na-a-dug$_4$
4. še-ba ur-lugal-ka
5. guru$_7$-a a-na mu-un-tag$_4$-a
6. ḫa-mu-na-ab-šúm-mu
7. nam-mi-ni-íb-tag$_4$-tag$_4$

Tell Shesh-kala and Lu-Nanna to give him (i.e., the bearer of this tablet) the grain rations of Ur-lugal, as much as is left over in the granary. (Tell) him not to leave anything there!

195. TCS 1 231 (BM 25368)

1. ur-^{d}lama-ra
2. ù-na-a-dug$_{4}$
3. še é a-tu-a
4. ba-an-da-ág-a-a
5. še ḫé-bar-re
6. na-mi-gur-re

Tell Ur-Lama to release the grain that was measured out in the house of Atu. (The matter) must not come up again!

196. TCS 1 253 (YOS 4 125)

1. ur-^{d}nin-su
2. ù-na-dug$_{4}$
3. a-šà ^{I}ummeda
4. 4 (bùr) GÁNA-àm
5. šà-bi-ta
6. 2 (bùr) GÁNA-àm
7. ku-li in-uru$_{4}$
8. 2 (bùr) GÁNA-àm
9. lú in-uru$_{4}$-a-bi
10. ummeda-ra ḫé-na-ab-pàd-dè

Tell Ur-Ninsu: The wetnurse (or: Ummeda) has a field of four bur, of which Kuli has cultivated (an area of) two bur. (Tell) him to find someone to cultivate the (other) two bur for the wetnurse (or: for Ummeda).

197. TCS 1 219 (ITT 3 5213)

1. ur-gar-ra
2. ù-na-a-dug$_{4}$
3. 20.0.0 še gur
4. lú-dug$_{4}$-níg-sa$_{6}$-ga-ra
5. ḫé-na-ab-šúm-mu
6. dub ur-gu-la-mu-bi
7. šà-ba ḫé-na-a-gá-gá
8. 30.0.0 še gur
9. a-ḫu-ki-in
10. ḫé-na-ab-šúm-mu
11. dub-ba-ni šu na-ba-ši-íb-ti-gá
12. še-bi ḫé-dadag
13. giš-bi si ḫé-ab-sá

Tell Ur-gar to give Lu-dugnisaga 6,000 liters of grain and to credit this to the account (lit., tablet) of Ur-gulamu.

(Tell) him to give Ahu-kin 9000 liters of grain, without letting him receive his tablet, to *clear* that grain (account) and to put in order its *wood (account)*.

198. TCS 1 225 (TCS 1 pl. 12)

1. ur-^{d}ig-alim
2. ù-na-a-dug$_4$
3. zíz gig ša-lim-be-lí in-de$_6$-a
4. numun-šè
5. 3 (bùr) GÁNA-kam
6. lú-bi-mu
7. ḫé-na-ab-šúm-mu
8. su$_{13}$-ga-r[a]
9. 1 (bùr) GÁNA kisiga^{ki}-šè
10. ḫé-na-ab-šúm-mu

Tell Ur-Igalim to give Lu-bimu emmer (and) wheat from the (grain) delivered by Shalim-beli; it is for seed for a field of three bur.

(Tell) him to give Suga one bur of land in the vicinity of (the town of) Kisiga.

199. TCS 1 198 (TCS 1 pl. 10)

1. puzur$_4$-ḫa-ià
2. ù-na-a-dug$_4$
3. 60.0.0 še gur
4. ki dumu in-si-na^{ki}-ke$_4$-ne-ta
5. ù še sag$_{11}$-ni
6. mu ^{d}en-líl-lá-šè
7. ⌜še⌝-munu$_4$-šè
8. šu-bal-a
9. ḫé-ma-ke$_4$
10. na-mi-gur-re
11. e$_4$-ma-ru-kam

Tell Puzur-Haja to exchange 18,000 liters of grain that (had come in) from the citizens of Isin, as well as grain that is (from) his harvest, for malt on behalf of Enlila. (The matter) must not come up again! It is urgent!

200. TCS 1 199 (TCS 1 pl. 10)

1. puzur$_4$-ha-ià
2. ù-na-a-dug$_4$
3. 40.0.0 še gur
4. i-dì-èr-ra
5. šu-bal-a
6. ḫé-mu-na-ak-e
7. e$_4$-ma-ru-kam
8. na-mi-gur-re

Tell Puzur-Haja to exchange 12,000 liters of grain with Iddin-Erra. It is urgent! (The matter) must not come up again!

201. TCS 1 22 (TCS 1 pl. 1)

1. al-la
2. ù-na-a-dug$_4$
3. še níg-⌜gál⌝-la
4. lugal-⌜ú⌝-šim-e
5. in-da-gál-la-aš
6. gá-da nu-me-a
7. na-ba-an-dù

Tell Alla that he must not withhold without my permission the grain, the property that is presently with Lugal-ushime.

202. TCS 1 23 (Fish, *JRAS* 1939:615)

1. al-la-ra
2. ù-na-a-dug$_4$
3. lá-u$_x$(NI) é ^{d}ba-Ú-ka
4. šu ḫa-ab-bar-re
5. ù lú-gar
6. ḫa-na-zi-zi

Tell Alla to release the leftover amounts from (the accounts of) the temple of Ba'u and to debit (this to the account of) Lu-gar.

203. AUCT 1 561

1. 0.0.3 zíd sig$_{15}$
2. 0.0.1.5 sìla eša
3. šar-ru-ba-ni
4. ḫé-na-ab-⌜šúm⌝-mu

(Tell) Sharrum-bani to give him 30 liters of coarse flour (and) fifteen liters of esha-flour.

204. TCS 1 373 (TCS 1 pl. 21)
(Akkadian)

1. *a-na*
2. ur-^{d}nin-si$_4$-an-na
3. *qí-bí-ma*
4. 2 SÌLA Ì.GIŠ
5. *šu-bí-lam*
6. KIŠIB ip-qú-ša

Seal: ip-qú-ša
dub-sar
dumu ku-ku-sà-num

Speak to Ur-Ninsiana: Send me two liters of sesame oil! Seal of Ipqusha.

Seal: Ipqusha, scribe, son of Kukusanum.

205. TCS 1 142 (Ni 2084)

1. lugal-ezen-ra
2. ù-na-a-dug$_4$
3. amar-šuba munu$_4$-mú
4. lú-^{d}nin-šubur-ka-ra
5. lú ì-giš na-bí-zi-zi
6. á-ága sanga-kam
7. tukum-bi
8. giš nu-ra-tuk-ga?
9. é-a-ni gul-a

Seal: lugal-nam-tar-[re]
dub-sar
dumu úr-ra-DINGIR
gu-za-lá

Tell Lugal-ezen that no one is to issue sesame oil to the maltster Amar-shuba, a man of Lu-Ninshubur! These are the instructions of the chief temple administrator! Should anyone not heed you, destroy his house!

Seal: Lugal-namtare, scribe, son of Urra-ilum, the chair bearer.

206. TCS 1 371 (TCS 1 pl. 21)
(Akkadian)

1. *a-na* ^{d}en-líl-ì-sa$_6$
2. *qí-bí-ma*
3. 1.1.0 SU$_{11}$.LUM GUR
4. *a-na* nu-úr-^{d}IŠKUR
5. *i-din*
6. ⌜*a*⌝*-pu-tum*
7. *[la t]u-ma-sú*

Seal: ur-^{d}en-líl-lá
dumu ur-mes
dam-gàr

Speak to Enlil-isa: Give Nur-Adad 360 liters of dates. It is urgent! Do not *go against* him!

Seal: Ur-Enlila, son of Ur-mes, the merchant.

Letters Concerning Animals

207. TCS 1 52 (YOS 4 127)

1. da-da-ga
2. ù-na-a-dug$_4$
3. 1 ème máḫ
4. 1 dùr giš
5. mu-de$_6$ ^{d}šára-ta
6. lugal-kù-ga-ni
7. ḫé-na-ab-šúm-mu
8. dub-ba-ni šu ḫa-ba-ši-íb-ti-gá

Tell Dadaga to give Lugal-kugani a mature she-ass and a stud-ass from the deliveries to the temple (of the god) Shara, and to take his receipt.

208. TCS 1 121 (YOS 4 116)

1. lú-^{d}nin-šubur-ra
2. ù-na-a-dug$_4$
3. gud-mu
4. ^{giš}kiri$_6$ é-duru$_5$ lú-igi-ma-šè-ka
5. ú ḫé-en-gu$_7$-e
6. a-na-aš-àm
7. ur-^{d}lama-ke$_4$
8. ú gu$_7$-dè
9. nu-ub-še-ge
10. ù ^{giš}gána-ùr 1-àm
11. ur-saḫar-^{d}ba-Ú-ra
12. ḫa-na-ab-šúm-mu

Tell Lu-Ninshubur to graze my oxen in the orchard of the hamlet of Lu-igimashe. Why does Ur-Lama not allow them to graze?

Moreover, (tell him) to give a single harrow to Ur-sahar-Ba'u.

209. MVN 4 182

1. ur-⌜nigar⌝^{gar}-ra
2. ù-na-dug$_4$
3. udu lugal-^{giš}gigir$_x$(LAGAB × MU)-r[e] min-a-ba
4. šu ḫé-na-a-du$_8$-e
5. inim énsi-ka-ta-àm

Tell Ur-nigar to hold back both sheep of Lugal-gigir. It is by order of the governor!

210. MVN 11 3

1. ur-^{d}nanše
2. ù-na-a-dug$_4$
3. 1 gud èš-èš
4. UN-íl sagi-ra
5. ḫé-na-ab-šúm-mu
6. ud sakar iti šu-numun-ka-šè
7. mu ús-sa ki-maš^{ki} mu
   ús-sa-a-b[i]

Tell Ur-Nanshe to give Unil, the cupbearer, one festival ox. It is for the (celebrations of the) new moon in the month of Shunumuna (=Lagash month 4, Girsu month 7).

The year after (the year in which) Kimash (was defeated), the year after that (=Shulgi year 48).

211. Michalowski, *JCS* 28:166 no. 2

1. ḫu-nu-nu-ur
2. ù-na-a-dug$_4$
3. 1 sila$_4$
4. za-ti-ru-um-ra
5. ḫé-na-ab-šúm-mu

Seal: du$_{11}$-ga
dumu lú-^{d}nin-gír-su
sipa na-kab-tum

Tell Hununur to give Za-Tirum one lamb.

Seal: Duga, son of Lu-Ningirsu, the shepherd of the nakkabtum enclosure.

212. Michalowski, *JCS* 28:167 no. 3

1. lugal-nanga
2. ù-na-a-dug$_4$
3. 1 gún síg ùz
4. ur-^{d}nin-girima-ka
5. ⌜ḫé-mu-na-šúm-mu⌝
6. na-mi-gur-⌜re⌝
7. inim šabra-kam

Tell Lugal-nanga to give Ur-Ningirima one talent of goat hair. (The matter) must not come up again! It is the order of the prefect!

213. Owen, *OrNS* 40:392

1. lú-urub$_x$(URU × KÁR)^{ki}
2. ù-na-a-dug$_4$
3. 80 udu máš ḫi-a
4. na-sa$_6$-ke$_4$
5. ḫé-na-ab-šúm-mu
6. 30 gún síg
7. bar-ta ì-gál
8. ^{d}utu-gír-gal-ra
9. ḫé-na-ab-bé
10. ḫa-ba-an-tùm

Seal: ^{d}šul-gi
nita kala-ga
lugal uri$_5$^{ki}-ma
lugal an ub-da límmu-ba
^{d}lama-palil
rá-gaba
ára[d-zu]

Tell Lu-Urub to give Nasa 80 assorted sheep and goats, (but) he has to promise to bring Utu-girgal 30 talents of wool that has been reserved (for him).

Seal: O Shulgi, mighty male, king of Ur, king of the four quarters of the universe—Lama-palil, the equerry, is your servant!

214. Owen, *OrNS* 40:389

1. [x?-b]u-ú
2. ù-na-a-dug$_4$
3. im-sar è-a
4. nam-šabra ur-nigar^{gar}
5. gud 15-ba
6. ù-bí-íb-bé
7. [š]u ḫé-em-ús-e
8. [mu lugal-á-z]i-da-šè

Tell X-bu to dispatch to me the account(s) of expenditures (issued) during the prefecture of Ur-nigar concerning the fifteen oxen. It is on behalf of Lugal-azida.

215. MVN 3 352

1. za-zi-ra
2. ù-na-a-dug$_4$
3. 1 u$_8$ sig$_5$
4. dingir-bi-mu
5. ḫé-na-ab-šúm-mu
6. na-bí-gur-re

Seal: ur-[x]
dumu la-na ⌜kurušda⌝

Tell Zazi to give Dingir-bimu one high quality ewe. (The matter) must not come up again!

Seal: Ur-[x], son of Lana, the animal fattener.

216. MVN 1 253

1. ur-mes
2. ù-na-a-dug$_4$
3. 60 udu máš du$_{10}$-ga
4. a-ḫu-ni-ši
5. ḫé-na-ab-šúm-mu
6. na-mi-gur-re

Seal: du$_{11}$-ga dub-sar
dumu lú-^{d}nin-gír-su
sipa udu na-kab-tum

Tell Ur-mes to give Ahu-nishi 60 *good quality* sheep and goats. (The matter) must not come up again!

Seal: Duga, scribe, son of Lu-Ningirsu, the shepherd of the sheep of the nakkabtum enclosure.

217. TCS 1 346 (TCS 1 pl. 19)

1. 4 udu máš-ḫi-a
2. ki wa-wa-ti
3. ù la-núm-ta
4. du$_{11}$-ga ì-dab$_5$
5. a-ba šeš-mu-gin$_7$
6. na-mi-gur-re
7. iti šu-eš$_5$-ša
8. mu ^{d}šu-^{d}sìn lugal

Seal: du$_{11}$-ga
dub-sar
dumu lú-^{d}nin-gír-su

Duga has received four assorted sheep and goats from Wawati and Lanum. Who is (as good) as my brother? (The matter) must not come up again!
Month of Shueshsha (= Drehem month 8). The year that Shu-Sin became king.

Seal: Duga, scribe, son of Lu-Ningirsu.

218. TCS 1 280 (TCS 1 pl. 16)

1. ur-tum-al
2. ù-na-a-dug$_4$
3. gud ur-gi$_4$-gi$_4$
4. a-šà-ga a-ab-gub
5. lugal á zi-ga-na
6. šu ḫé-ba-re
7. [e$_4$]-ma-ru-kam
8. [na]-mi-gur-[r]e

Seal: ur-^{d}nin-mú
dub-sar
dumu [. . .]

Tell Ur-Tummal that Ur-gigi's ox is out in the field (and) that *the person who wronged him* must release it. It is urgent! (The matter) must not come up again!

Seal: Ur-Ninmu, scribe, son of . . .

219. TCS 1 282 (UDT 32)

1. ur-tur-ra
2. ù-na-a-dug$_4$
3. en-na zú-si-šè
4. lugal-mè-a
5. mu udu lá-u$_x$(NI)-šè
6. ka na-ì-ba-e
7. dub-ba-ni šu ḫa-ba-ab-ti

Tell Ur-tur that Lugal-mea must not open his mouth to anyone about the missing sheep until the shearing. (Tell) him to receive his tablet.

220. TCS 1 29 (ITT 2 3418)

1. an-na-ḫi-li-bi
2. ù-na-a-dug$_4$
3. 10 adda udu
4. ur-^{d}ḫendur-sag-ra
5. ḫé-na-ab-šúm-mu
6. ud na-bí-íb-zal-e

Seal: lú-kal-la
dub-sar
dumu ur-^{d}ḫendur-sag$^{?}$

Tell Anna-hilibi to give ten sheep carcasses to Ur-Hendursaga, (and) that not (even one) day must pass!

Seal: Lu-kala, scribe, son of Ur-Hendursaga.

Miscellaneous Letters

221. TCS 1 296 (STR 18)

1. šeš-kal-la
2. ù-na-a-dug$_4$
3. 4 ^{giš}ad
4. 2 ^{giš}tu-gul-bi
5. 2 ^{giš}zú-ba
6. ur-mes-ra
7. ḫa-mu-na-ab-šúm-mu
8. na-mi-gú-re
9. mu ^{d}amar-^{d}sìn lugal

Seal: árad-mu
dub-sar
dumu ur-nigar^{gar} kuš$_7$

Tell Shesh-kala to give Ur-mes four *stern planks,* two *posts,* and two . . . (The matter) must not come up again! The year that Amar-Sin became king (= Amar-Sin year 1).

Seal: Arad-mu, scribe, son of Ur-nigar, the equerry.

222. TCS 1 355 (TCS 1 pl. 19)

1. 30 gún ésir ḫád
2. ésir ḫád dar-gu-la-ke$_4$
3. ḫa-ba-ab-daḫ-e
4. gá-e ga-na-ab-su

(Tell) him to add 30 talents of dry bitumen to the dry bitumen (already assigned) for the (boat) mast. I myself will return it to him!

223. TCS 1 372 (TLB 3 66) (Akkadian)

1. *a-na* eš$_4$-tár-dan-na-at
2. *qí-bí-ma*
3. 3 ^{túg}GUZ.ZA 4.KAM-ÚS
4. 3 ^{túg}BAR.DUL$_5$ GIN
5. Ì ^{giš}EREN
6. Ì [DU$_{10}$].GA [GÍB]IL
7. Ì S[U$_{11}$.L]UM
8. *la-aš-[šu-ú]*
9. *šu-bi-⌜li-im⌝*

Seal: á-da-gin?-na
sag-du$_5$ [?]
dumu ^{d}en-líl-[. . .]

Speak to Eshtar-dannat: I do not have three fourth-quality guza garments, three ordinary cloaks, (or any) cedar oil, fresh sweet oil, (or) date oil. Send me (these things)!

Seal: Adagina, field registrar . . . , son of Enlil-. . . .

224. AUCT 3 323

1. za-ti-ru-um
2. ù-na-a-dug$_4$
3. 1 ^{giš}kum
4. šu šúm-mu-dè
5. lugal-kù-zu
6. gú ba-an-dé
7. šu ḫé-bar-re

Seal: ^{d}i-bí-^{d}sìn
dingir kalam-ma-na
lugal kala-ga
lugal uri$_5$^{ki}-ma
^{d}sìn-ba-ni
muḫaldim
dumu i-ti-a
árad-zu

Tell Za-Tirum to release one wooden mortar which was to be entrusted to Lugal-kuzu, but which has been lost.

Seal: O Ibbi-Sin, god of his land, mighty king, king of Ur—Sin-bani, the cook, son of Itija, is your servant!

225. NATN 971

1. ur-^{d}sìn-ra
2. ù-na-a-dug$_4$
3. tukum-bi
4. ab-ba-a šeš bàn-da
5. zi lugal in-na-an-pàd
6. nam-engar-šè
7. šeš gal-e šeš bàn-da
8. zi lugal in-na-an-pàd
9. nam-engar šeš bàn-da ḫé-na-ab-šúm-mu

Say to Ur-Sin: Should the father swear by the name of the king on behalf of the younger son (and) the older son swear by the name of the king on behalf of the younger son concerning the status of tenant farmer, he is then to make the younger son into a tenant farmer.

226. MVN 3 332

1. ba-gi-na
2. ù-na-dug$_4$
3. nu-úr-zu-⸢e⸣
4. na-ab-be$_8$-a
5. kin lugal-pa-è
6. ù-mu-gíd
7. dub-ba-ni ḫa-mu-na-ab-šúm-mu
8. na-mi-gur-re
9. a-ba šeš-mu-gin$_7$

Seal: nu-úr-zu
árad ^{d}en-líl-lá

Tell Bagina—thus says Nur-Zu—that when Lugal-pae has finished his work, he is to hand over to him his (debt) tablet. (The matter) must not come up again! Who is (as good) as my brother?

Seal: Nur-Zu, servant of (the god) Enlil.

227. Yoshikawa, *ASJ* 6:127

1. ur-é-maš-ra
2. ù-na-a-dug$_4$
3. 60 giš-ùr
4. la-ma-ša sukkal
5. ḫé-na-ab-šúm-mu
6. má-a ḫa-mu-na-gá-gá
7. 3 guruš-àm
8. m[á ḫ]é-da-gíd
9. [. . .]-dè
10. [. . .]-bal-šè
11. [. . .]^{ki}-ta
12. [. . .]-a-šè

Tell Ur-Emash to give the envoy Lamasha 60 roof-beams; that they are to be put on a boat, and that three workers are to haul the boat. . . . from place [A] to place [B].

228. MVN 15 371

1. [. . .]
2. [ù-n]a-a-dug$_4$
3. 20 ^{giš}mi-rí-za úr
4. ur-^{d}šu-maḫ
5. [ḫ]é-na-ab-šúm-mu

Tell [so-and-so] to give Ur-Shumah 20 *(boat) keel planks.*

229. MVN 15 375

1. nam-ḫa-ni-[ra?]
2. ù-na-a-d[ug$_4$]
3. 300.0.0 gur in-u
4. ḫa-mu-na-[ab]-šúm-mu
5. na-mi-gu[r-re]
6. ⌜é⌝ ^{d}i[nanna]

Seal: ur-nigar^{gar}
dub-sar
dumu ur-sukkal
nu-bànda éren-na-ka

Tell Namhani to give him 90,000 liters of straw. (The matter) must not come up again!

Subscript: The temple of (the goddess) Inanna.

Seal: Ur-nigar, scribe, son of Ur-sukkal, the captain of the troops.

230. Owen, *Or*NS 40:387

1. lugal-á-zi-da
2. ù-na-a-dug$_4$
3. 0.0.3 naga
4. ḫé-na-šúm-mu

Seal: ^{d}i-bí-^{d}sìn
lugal kala-ga
lugal uri$_5^{ki}$-ma

^{d}šul-gi-^{d}utu$^{[ši]}$
àga-uš g[al-gal]
dumu ni-g[u?]
árad-zu

Tell Lugal-azida to give him (the bearer of this message) 30 liters of alkali.

Seal: O Ibbi-Sin, mighty king, king of Ur, Shulgi-Shamshi, the chief constable, son of Nigu, is your servant!

231. Owen, *Or*NS 40:390

1. 1 ba-rí-ga
2. [s]ag-ba urudu gar-ra
3. ki ur-^{d}šul-pa-è dub-sar-ta
4. mu-de$_6$
5. šeš-kal-la
6. ù-na-a-dug$_4$
7. dub-ba-ni
8. šu ḫé-bí-bar-re

Seal: ur-^{d}[. . .]
nu-bànda [x]

One bariga-(measure vessel) whose cover is inlaid with copper was delivered from the scribe Ur-Shulpae. Tell Shesh-kala to release his account.

Seal: Ur-[. . .], inspector of [. . .]

232. Owen, *OrNS* 40:391

1. šeš-sa$_6$-⌜ga⌝
2. ù-na-a-⌜dug$_4$⌝
3. 0.0.3 kaš sig$_5$
4. ku-bu-du$_7$
5. ḫa-mu-na-šúm-mu

Seal: ka$_5$[a]
dub-sar
dumu ur-^{d}lugal-bàn-da

Tell Shesh-saga to give Kubudu 30 liters of good beer.

Seal: Ka, scribe, son of Ur-Lugalbanda.

233. TCS 1 56 (BM 107873)

1. dingir-ra
2. ù-na-a-dug$_4$
3. 35 gu-nígin níg-ki-luḫ-ḫa
4. é-gal má-a ḫé-em-gá-gá
5. ^{d}en-líl-lá-ì-sa$_6$
6. ur-^{d}utu
7. ù 20 guruš nu-^{giš}kiri$_6$
8. ḫé-em-da-ab-gi$_4$-gi$_4$
9. ú-la-bi u$_4$-te-ta gi$_6$-ba-šè
10. 1.0.0 su$_{11}$-lum sig$_5^!$ gur
11. sá-dug$_4$ lugal ḫé-ma-da-tùm

Tell Dingira to load the boat with 35 packets of brooms for the palace, and to send to me Enlil-isa, Ur-Utu, and 20 gardeners, and moreover, to bring to me, quickly, before daybreak (lit., from day to midnight), 300 liters of fine dates as the regular royal offering.

234. TCS 1 87 (ITT 5 6975)

1. kù-nin-a-na
2. ù lugal-amar-kù-ra
3. ù-ne-a-dug$_4$
4. pisan [dub]-ba
5. nibru^{ki}-ta
6. ì-de$_6$-a
7. [ur-^{d}i]g-alim
8. dub-sar pisan-dub-ba-ra
9. ḫé-na-ab-šúm-mu
10. na-mi-gur-re
11. e$_4$-ma-ru-kam

Tell Ku-Nina and Lugal-amarku to give Ur-Igalim, scribe and chief accountant, the tablet-basket that had been delivered from Nippur. (The matter) must not come up again! It is urgent!

235. TCS 1 113 (Gomi—Sato 222)

1. lú-nam-tar-ra
2. ù-na-a-dug$_4$
3. a-kal-la ù lú-uru-sag-ra
4. en-na igi-mu-šè
5. di in-da-an-du$_{11}$-ga-aš
6. na-ba-dù
7. ḫa-àm-DU
8. inim énsi-kam
9. ù a-šà uru-ul-ka
10. á-bi in-da-ág-e
11. zi lugal ḫé-an-pàd
12. u$_4$ nu-mu-zal-e

Tell Lu-namtar not to detain Aja-kala and Lu-urusag until they have presented their case before me. It is the order of the governor, *let them go!* And furthermore, he must swear by the name of the king that he will pay the rent of the Uru-ul field (or: the field at Uru ul/"Old Town"). Not (even) one day must pass!

236. TCS 1 257 (TCS 1 pl. 15)

1. ur-^{d}nun-gal-ra
2. ù-na-a-dug$_4$
3. 3.0.0 kaš ninda gur
4. 2 udu niga
5. 3 udu ú
6. 1 ^{túg}níg-lám 3-kam-⌜ús⌝
7. 10 ^{túg}guz-za 3-kam-⌜ús⌝
8. 10 ^{túg}sag uš-bar
9. 5.0.0 su$_{11}$-lum gur
10. ḫu-lí-bar-r[a]
11. ḫé-na-ab-šúm-mu

Tell Ur-Nungal to give Hulibar 900 liters of beer-bread, two fattened sheep, three grazed sheep, one third-grade niglam-garment, ten third-grade guza-garments, ten first-quality garments from the weavers, and 1,500 liters of dates.

237. Owen, *Or*NS 40:400
(Akkadian)

1. *a-na* DINGIR-mu-ta-[bil]
2. *qí-bí-ma*
3. ŠE.MUNU$_4$ BAPPIR
4. *ša i-ri-šu-kà*
5. ⌜*a*⌝*-na* šu-èr-⌜ra⌝

Rest broken

Speak to Ilum-muttabbil: . . . the beer-malt that he asked you about. . . . to Shu-Erra . . .

238. Michalowski, *JCS* 28:167 no. 1

1. ur-mes-ra
2. ù-na-a-dug_4
3. á má ḫun-gá
4. má bal-a-ke_4
5. sá nu-na-da-ab-du_{11}-ga
6. šà-ni bí-tam
7. ur-mes-ra
8. ḫé-na-ab-zi-zi

Tell Ur-mes that it has not been possible to deliver to him directly the rent for the hired boat which has (already) been unloaded. He hired (the boat) on credit. (Tell) him to credit it to Ur-mes.

239. Michalowski, *JCS* 28:167 no. 4

1. 0.0.2 ì
2. 3 sìla ì-nun
3. 1 ⌜sìla⌝ làl
4. 1 udu niga
5. 1 udu ú
6. 1 ku_6 $še_6$ gur
7. ù-ma-ni
8. ù-na-a-dug_4
9. e_4-ma-ru-kam
10. ul_4-la-bi
11. ur-^{d}nin-gidri nar
12. ḫé-na-ab-šúm-mu

Twenty liters of oil, three liters of ghee, one liter of date syrup, one fattened sheep, one grazed sheep, (and) 300 liters of smoked fish. Tell Umani that it is urgent that he quickly give these (goods) to Ur-Nin-gidri, the cantor.

240. Neumann, *AoF* 19:31-32

This letter is quite fragmentary but it is of special interest as it is known only in a copy made sometime during the first millennium in the city of Babylon. The scribe imitated the old Ur III hand and added a colophon in archaizing late script. According to this subscript the original letter was found in the Ekishnugal, the temple of the moon god Sin in Ur. There is no way of establishing if this is a copy of a real letter, or a late fabrication. Because only a central part of the tablet has been preserved, the text is difficult to understand.

Column i

1. [. . .] x [. . .] x-lá
2. [. . . ^{d}s]ìn-ke$_4$
3. [na-b]é-a
4. [$^{(d)}$šu]l-gi
5. [lu]gal-mu
6. ⌜ù⌝-na-a-dug$_4$
7. ⌜é⌝ dingir-re-e-ne-ke$_4$
8. [. . .]-ba

Column ii

1. ga-b[a-x]
2. še ba x[. . .]
3. ga-b[a-x]
4. gud-e [. . .] ga-ba-[x]
5. ^{giš}api[n x]
6. lú g[i$_4$-bí]-í[b- . . .]
7. sipa [. . .]
8. udu e$^{?}$ [. . .] x [. . .]

Column 3

1′. šuku [. . .]
2′. 1 (bùr) GÁNA-t[a-àm]
3′. sag g[a- . . .]
4′. šakkan[a énsi-ke$_4$]-e-ne
5′. éren-na-ne-n[e]
6′. šuku gi$_4$-b[í]-íb-[x]
7′. ^{d}šul-g[i . . .]

Column 4

1′. *[ki]*-⌜*i*⌝ KA *ṭup-pi* SUMUN
2′. *[ša]* ⌜é⌝-giš-nu$_{11}$-gal
3′. *[ša-ṭi]r-ma ba-ár*
4′. [ŠU ^{m} . . .]-ba-^{d}marduk
5′. [DUMU ^{m} . . .]-^{d}marduk MAŠ.MAŠ
6′. [A ^{m} . . .]x-^{d}marduk
7′. *[ina q]ì-bit*
8′. [. . .] ⌜*ú*⌝-*kin*

lower edge

1′. [. . . K]Á.DINGIR.MEŠ⌜^{ki}⌝ [. . .]
2′. [. . . *qa-t]i*

Tell His Majesty, (King) Shulgi: Thus says . . . , the . . . of Mr. . . . -Sin: The temples of the gods . . .

I want to . . . , I want to . . . the grain rations of the . . . I want to . . . oxen of . . . . Someone must return . . . plow(s) . . . shepherd(s) . . . sheep . . .

The subsistence plots of the . . . at one bur of land each . . . I want to . . . Give subsistence plots to the generals [and the governors] and their conscripts! (King) Shulgi . . .

Written and checked according to the wording of an original tablet from the Ekishnugal (temple). Hand of . . .-Marduk, son of . . .-Marduk, the exorcist priest, descendant of . . .-Marduk. By command of . . . I placed it in . . . .

. . . Babylon . . . , finished.

IV

Letters from the Time of the Dynasty of Isin

The Third Dynasty of Ur overextended its reach and built up a shaky administrative system that could not survive for more than a century. Eventually, the state structure disintegrated, and the last king of the dynasty, Ibbi-Sin, reigned only over Ur and the surrounding countryside. A military officer in his employ, Ishbi-Erra, who apparently came from Mari, took advantage of the weakness of the central government and, after being appointed governor of Isin and Nippur, managed to secure independence and set up a kingdom in Isin. Foreigners from the east eventually raided Sumer and Akkad and occupied Ur. According to native literary tradition, Ibbi-Sin was led off in chains to Iran, where he died in captivity. The Ur III state was no more, but the new rulers of Isin made every attempt to emulate their former employers and claimed to be the heirs to the kings of Ur. Only four letters have survived from the early years of the Isin dynasty, from the reigns of its founder Ishbi-Erra (2017–1985 BCE), its fourth ruler Ishme-Dagan (1953–1935), and its fifth king Lipit-Eshtar (1934–1924). The order of the year names of the early Isin dynasty is uncertain; the designations used here follow Sigrist (1988).

The last text in this collection, from the time of Lipit-Eshtar, is the last known archival letter in the Sumerian language.

241. BIN 9 475
(Akkadian)

1. *a-na* puzur$_4$-ki-iš
2. *qí-bí-ma*
3. 2.2.0 GUR SI-*na-am*
4. *šu-bi-lá-am*
5. KI tu-ra-am-ì-lí
6. šu-eš$_4$-tár
7. ŠU BA.TI

Seal: šu-[eš$_4$-tá]r?
⌜dumu⌝ [. . .]

Tell Puzur-Kish: Send me 420 liters of . . . . Shu-Eshtar received it from Turam-ili.

Seal: Shu-Eshtar, son of . . . .

242. BIN 9 486

1. 2 ^{dug}ŠÀ.KI
2. zíd še-gín-šè
3. ^{d}nanna-ki-ág
4. ⌜ḫé-na-ab-šúm⌝-mu
5. iti ⌜šu-numun⌝-a
6. mu ús-sa šu-nir gal ^{d}inanna ba-dím

(Tell so-and-so) to give Nanna-kiaga two *jars* for flour and glue (mixture).

Month of Shunumuna (= month 4).

The year after (the year) in which the great emblem of Inanna was fashioned (Ishbi-Erra year 21).

243. NBC 8863

1. šà-tam-e-ne
2. ù-ne-a-dug$_4$
3. 1 sag géme
4. èr-ra-ba-ni
5. nibru^{ki}-ta ⌜è⌝-a
6. šu ḫé-bar-re
7. iti šu-numun-a
8. mu ^{d}iš-me-^{d}da-gan [lugal-e] en ^{d}nanna [ur]i$_5$^{ki} [i]n-pàd

Tell the shatam-officials to release the slave girl of Erra-bani who came up from Nippur.

Month of Shunumuna (= month 4).

The year that (king) Ishme-Dagan appointed (by omen) the high priestess of (the god) Nanna in Ur (= Ishme-Dagan year B).

244. YOS 14 317

1. ur-^{d}nin-urta ka-gur$_7$
2. ù šà-tam-e-ne
3. ù-ne-a-dug$_4$
4. 10.0.0 še x [gur]
5. 40 [. . .] 10 x [. . .]
6. 6 túg x [. . .]
7. bur-^{d}IŠKUR
8. sá-dug$_4$-šè
9. ḫa-ba-ab-šúm-mu-ne
10. dub-a-ni šu ḫa-ab-ti-gá:ne
11. iti gud-s[i]-su
12. mu ^{d}li-[pí-i]t-eš$_4$-tár
13. lugal-e inim ^{d}en-líl
14. ^{d}nanna-ta uri$_5$^{ki}
15. ki-bi b[í-i]n-gi$_4$-a

Seal: [. . .]
[. . .]
lugal [. . .]
[. . .]
[. . .]
dub-sar
dumu x-^{d}amar-^{d}sìn-ka
árad-[zu]

Tell Ur-Ninurta and the shatam-officials to give 3,000 liters of grain, forty . . . , ten . . . , six garments . . . to Bur-Adad for the regular deliveries (and) to receive his receipt.

Month of Gudsisu (= month 2).

The year that king Lipit-Eshtar restored Ur by command of (the god) Enlil and of (the god) Nanna. (Lipit-Eshtar year B).

Seal: [O (king) so-and-so, . . . ,] king of . . . , [so-and-so], scribe, son of . . .-Amar-Sin, is [your] servant!

Sources

Original handcopies or first editions are indicated at the heading of each translated letter in the main portion of the book. Basic textual editions, not necessarily the original publications, are listed below. The number of each entry corresponds to the number assigned to letters in the book.

1. **Edition:** Thureau-Dangin 1907; Grégoire 1962: 9–10. **Translation:** Kramer 1963: 331.
2. **Edition:** Pettinato 1977a: 239–40; Pettinato 1991: 240–41; Platt 1988: 247-48 (partial).
3. **Edition:** Pettinato 1980; Edzard 1981. **Translation:** Liverani 1988: 214.
4. **Edition:** Sollberger 1954: 30; Volk 1992: 24–26.
5. **Edition:** Thureau-Dangin 1910: 6.
8. **Edition:** Westhuizen 1989: 280–81.
9. **Edition:** Westhuizen 1989: 279–80.
10. **Edition:** Westhuizen 1990: 261–62.
11. **Edition:** Thureau-Dangin 1910: 17.
12. **Edition:** Whiting 1972: 335.
13. **Edition:** Edzard 1968: 152.
15. **Edition:** Limet 1973: 78.
16. **Edition:** Limet 1973: 79.
17. **Edition:** Foster 1982c: 28–29.
18. **Edition:** Pettinato 1968: 173–74.
21. **Edition:** Thureau-Dangin 1926: 25–29. **Translation:** Oppenheim 1967: 71.
22. **Edition:** Smith 1932: 295–301; Foster 1990b: 31 (partial). **Translation:** Oppenheim 1967: 71–72; Laessøe 1963: 29 (partial).
23. **Edition:** Yang 1989: 127.
24. **Edition:** Whiting 1972: 334–35 (partial); Yang 1989: 125–26.
25. **Edition:** Yang 1989: 126–27.
26. **Edition:** Yang 1989: 129–30.
27. **Edition:** Yang 1989: 124–25.
28. **Edition:** Yang 1989: 127–28.
29. **Edition:** Yang 1989: 129.
30. **Edition:** Sollberger 1956a: 17–18; Yang 1989: 122–23.
31. **Edition:** Yang 1989: 126.

32. **Edition:** Yang 1989: 130.
33. **Edition:** Yang 1989: 128.
34. **Edition:** Meek 1935: xviii–xix.
35. **Edition:** Meek 1935: xix–xx.
36. **Edition:** Meek 1935: xx. **Translation:** Kraus 1975–76: 87.
37. **Edition:** Meek 1935: xxi.
38. **Edition:** Meek 1935: xxii.
39. **Edition:** Meek 1935: xxii.
40. **Copy:** Watelin and Langdon 1930: pl. 11.
41. **Edition:** Glassner 1986: 43 (partial). **Translation:** Gelb 1970: XVI (partial).
42. **Edition:** Whiting 1972: 336.
45. **Edition:** Foster 1977: 43 (partial).
47. **Edition:** Gelb 1955: 322–23.
48. **Edition:** Foster 1982b: 33.
49. **Edition:** Foster 1982b: 33.
50. **Edition:** Foster 1982b: 33–34.
51. **Copy:** Westenholz 1984: 79. **Edition:** Foster 1982a: 135–36.
52. **Edition:** Lambert 1975: 178; Foster 1982a: 136–37.
53. **Edition:** Pettinato 1968: 171–72.
54. **Edition:** Foster 1982a: 137.
55. **Edition:** Lambert 1975: 178.
56. **Edition:** Westhuizen 1989: 281–82.
57. **Edition:** Westhuizen 1989: 282–83.
58. **Edition:** Wilcke 1978: 211–12; Steinkeller 1984: 86–87 (partial).
59. **Edition:** Kraus 1975–76: 93 (partial); Westhuizen 1990: 263–64.
60. **Edition:** Westhuizen 1990: 264–65.
61. **Edition:** Westenholz 1974: 74–75.
62. **Edition:** Goetze 1947: 345–46.
63. **Edition:** Veenhof 1975–76: 105–7.
64. **Edition:** Lambert 1975: 163; Foster 1977: 41; Wilcke 1977.
65. **Edition:** Neumann 1988: 209–10.
66. **Edition:** Edzard 1968: 150–51.
67. **Edition:** Lambert 1965: 115; Edzard 1968: 150.
68. **Edition:** Lambert 1965: 115; Edzard 1968: 149.
69. **Edition:** Yoshikawa 1984: 125–26.
70. **Edition:** Foster 1982c: 106.
71. **Edition:** Steinkeller and Postgate 1992: 102.
78. **Edition:** Lafont 1987: 627.
89. **Edition:** Lafont 1990: 167–68.
90. **Seal inscription:** Lafont 1986: 76 = Lafont and Yıldız 1989: 113.
96. **Edition:** Ali 1964: 27–33; Ali 1970: 146–51; Michalowski 1976b: 135–46. **Translation:** Kramer 1963: 331–32.

97. **Edition:** Ali 1964: 34–41; Ali 1970: 152–59; Michalowski 1976b: 147–59. **Translation:** Kramer 1963: 332–33.
100. **Edition:** Hallo 1969: 174.
101. **Edition:** Touzalin 1982: 52.
109. **Edition:** Touzalin 1982: 92.
110. **Edition:** Touzalin 1982: 44.
111. **Edition:** Touzalin 1982: 47.
115. **Collation:** Waetzoldt 1976: 327.
116. **Edition:** Pettinato 1968: 176.
118. **Edition:** Owen 1971: 398–99.
120. **Collation:** Yıldız and Gomi 1988: 20.
121. **Edition:** Owen 1972: 133–34.
122. **Edition:** van de Mieroop 1984: 55–58.
124. **Edition:** Michalowski 1976a: 165.
132. **Edition:** Hallo 1969: 174.
134. **Edition:** Hallo 1969: 174.
137. **Edition:** Hallo 1969: 173–74.
138. **Edition:** Pettinato 1968: 169.
139. **Edition:** Pettinato 1968: 177; Pettinato and Waetzoldt 1985: 293.
140. **Edition:** Owen 1971: 388–89.
143. **Edition:** Owen 1971: 394.
155. **Edition:** Foster 1990a: 51–52.
168. **Edition:** Owen 1971: 396.
185. **Edition:** Lafont 1990: 168.
186. **Edition:** Lafont 1990: 167.
189. **Edition:** Hallo 1969: 174.
210. **Edition:** Michalowski 1976a: 164–65.
211. **Edition:** Michalowski 1976a: 162–63.
212. **Edition:** Michalowski 1976a: 163.
213. **Edition:** Owen 1971: 392–93.
214. **Edition:** Owen 1971: 389–90.
216. **Edition:** Pettinato 1968: 169–70.
227. **Edition:** Yoshikawa 1984: 121–24.
230. **Edition:** Owen 1971: 387–88.
231. **Edition:** Owen 1971: 390–91.
232. **Edition:** Owen 1971: 391.
237. **Edition:** Owen 1971: 400.
238. **Edition:** Michalowski 1976a: 161–62.
239. **Edition:** Hallo 1969: 175; Michalowski 1976a: 163–64.
240. **Edition:** Neumann 1992.
242. **Edition:** Hallo 1969: 175.
243. **Edition:** Hallo 1969: 175.
244. **Edition:** Sollberger 1966: 92. **Seal inscription:** Hallo 1969: 176.

Bibliography

Ali, Fadhil Abdulwahid

1964 "Sumerian Letters: Two Collections from the Old Babylonian Schools." Diss., University of Pennsylvania. Ann Arbor: University Microfilms.

1970 "Three Sumerian Letters," *Sumer* 26:145–78.

Alster, Bendt

1987 "A Note on the Uriah Letter in the Sumerian Sargon Legend," *Zeitschrift für Assyriologie* 77:169–73.

Böhl, Franz M. Th. de Liagre

1951 "Ein Brief des Königs Samsuiluna von Babylon (+/-1685-1648 v. Chr.)," *BO* 8:50–56.

Bridges, Susan Jane

1981 "The Mesag Archive: A Study of Sargonic Society and Economy." Diss., Yale University. Ann Arbor: University Microfilms.

Buchannan, Briggs

1981 *Early Near Eastern Seals in the Yale Babylonian Collection*. New Haven: Yale University Press.

Cagni, Luigi, and Giovanni Pettinato

1976 *Le collezioni del Biblico e di Aosta.* MVN 4. Rome: Multigrafia Editrice.

Cohen, Sol

1973 "Enmerkar and the Lord of Aratta." Diss., University of Pennsylvania. Ann Arbor: University Microfilms.

Cooper, Jerrold S., and Wolfgang Heimpel

1982 "The Sumerian Sargon Legend." *JAOS* 103: 67–82.

Cooper, Marc

1983 "Texts and Fragments." *JCS* 35: 197–98.

Crawford, Vaughn Emerson

1954 *Sumerian Economic Texts from the First Dynasty of Isin*. BIN 9. New Haven: Yale University Press.

Delaporte, Louis

1912 *Textes de l'époque d'Ur (Fouilles d'Ernest de Sarzec en 1898 et 1900).* ITT IV/1. Paris: Ernest Leroux.

Diakonoff, I. M.

1939 "Pis'mo k sumerskomu carju Šu-Sinu." *VDI* 1:59–64.

van Dijk, J.

1966 *The Archives of Nūršamaš and Other Loans.* TIM 3. Wiesbaden: Otto Harrassowitz.

1976 *Cuneiform Texts of Varying Content.* TIM 9. Leiden: Brill.

Donald, Trevor

1964 "Old Akkadian Tablets in the Liverpool Museum." *MCS* 9:230–307.

Donbaz, Veysel, and Benjamin R. Foster

1982 *Sargonic Texts from Telloh in the Istanbul Archaeological Museums.* Occasional Publications of the Babylonian Fund 5. Philadelphia: University Museum.

Durand, Jean-Marie

1982 *Documents cunéiformes de la IVe Section de l'École Pratique des Hautes Études. Tome I, Catalogue et copies cunéiformes.* Geneva/Paris: Librairie Droz.

Edzard, Dietz Otto

1968 *Sumerische Rechtsurkunden des III. Jahrtausends aus der Zeit vor der III. Dynastie von Ur.* Bayerische Akademie der Wissenschaften, Philosophisch-Historische Klasse, Abhandlungen, Neue Folge 67. Munich: Verlag der Bayerischen Akademie der Wissenschaften.

1981 "Neue Erwägungen zum Brief Enna-Dagan von Mari (TM.75.G.2367)." *Studi Eblaiti* 4:89–97.

Ellis, Maria deJong

1987 "The Goddess Kititum Speaks to King Ibalpiel: Oracle Texts from Ishchali." *M.A.R.I.: Annales de Recherches Interdisciplinaires* 5:235–66.

Figulla, Hugo Heinrich

1961 *Catalogue of the Babylonian Tablets in the British Museum, Volume I.* London: The British Museum.

Fish, Thomas

1939 "Two Sumerian Letters in the British Museum." *JRAS* 615–20.

1953 "Miscellany—Ur III." *MCS* 3:1–15.

1954 "Miscellaneous Texts." *MCS* 4:12–21.

Foster, Benjamin R.

1977 "Commercial Activity in Sargonic Mesopotamia." *Iraq* 39:31–43.

1982a *Umma in the Sargonic Period.* Memoirs of the Connecticut Academy of Arts and Sciences 20. Hamden: Archon Books.

1982b "An Agricultural Archive from Sargonic Akkad." *ASJ* 4:7–51.

1982c *Administration and Use of Institutional Land in Sargonic Sumer.* Mesopotamia 9. Copenhagen: Akademisk Forlag.

1982d "Administration of Land at Sargonic Gasur." *Oriens Antiquus* 21:39–48.

1990a "Two Late Old Akkadian Documents." *ASJ* 12:51–56.

1990b "The Gutian Letter Again." *Nouvelles Assyriologiques Brèves et Utilitaires* 31.

Gelb, Ignace J.

1952 *Sargonic Texts from the Diyala Region.* MAD 1. Chicago: University of Chicago Press.

1955 *Old Akkadian Inscriptions in Chicago Natural History Museum: Texts of Legal and Business Interest.* Fieldiana: Anthropology, 44/2. Chicago: Chicago Natural History Museum.

1970 *Sargonic Texts in the Ashmolean Museum, Oxford.* MAD 5. Chicago: University of Chicago Press.

Gelinas, Paul

1965 *History of the World for Young Readers.* New York: Grosset and Dunlap.

de Genouillac, Henri

1910 *Textes de l'époque d'Agadé et de l'époque d'Ur (Fouilles d'Ernest de Sarzec en 1894): Première partie.* ITT II/1. Paris: Ernest Leroux.

1911a *La Trouvaille de Dréhem: Étude avec un choix de textes de Constantinople et Bruxelles.* Paris: Paul Geuthner.

1911b *Textes de l'époque d'Agadé et de l'époque d'Ur (Fouilles d'Ernest de Sarzec en 1894): Deuxième partie.* ITT II/2. Paris: Ernest Leroux.

1921 *Époque présargonique, époque d'Agadé, époque d'Ur.* ITT V. Paris: Ernest Leroux.

Gibson, McGuire

1972 "Um El-Jir, A Town in Akkad," *JNES* 31:237–94.

Glassner, Jean-Jacques

1986 *La chute d'Akkadé: L'évènement et sa mémoire.* Berliner Beiträge zum Vorderen Orient 5. Berlin: Dietrich Reimer.

Goetze, Albrecht

1947 "Two Old Akkadian Tablets in St. Louis." *JCS* 1:345–48.

nd *Sumerian and Akkadian Texts.* YOS, Babylonian Texts 15. New Haven: Yale University Press.

Gomi, Tohru, and Susumu Sato

1990 *Selected Neo-Sumerian Administrative Texts from the British Museum.* Abiko: The Research Institute, Chuo-Gakuin University.

Grégoire, Jean-Pierre

1962 *La province méridionale de l'Etat de Lagash.* Luxembourg.

1981 *Inscriptions et archives administratives cunéiformes.* MVN 10. Rome: Multigrafia Editrice.

Guillén, Claudio

1986 "Notes Toward the Study of the Renaissance Letter." Pp. 70–101 in *Renaissance Genres: Essays on Theory, History, and Interpretation.* Ed. by Barbara Kiefer Lewalski. Harvard English Studies 14. Cambridge: Harvard University Press.

Hackman, George Gottlob

1958 *Sumerian and Akkadian Administrative Texts from Predynastic Times to the End of the Akkad Dynasty.* BIN 8. New Haven: Yale University Press.

Hallo, William W.

1963 *Sumerian Archival Texts.* TLB 3. Leiden: Nederlands Instituut voor het Nabije Oosten.

1968 "Individual Prayer in Sumerian: The Continuity of a Tradition." *JAOS* 88:71–89.

1969 "The Neo-Sumerian Letter-Orders." *BO* 26:171–76.

1972 "The House of Ur-Meme." *JNES* 31:87–95.

1981 "Letters, Prayers and Letter-Prayers." Pp. 17-27 in *Proceedings of the Seventh World Congress of Jewish Studies: Studies in the Bible and the Ancient Near East.* Jerusalem: World Union of Jewish Studies.

Keiser, Clarence Elwood

1919 *Selected Temple Documents of the Ur Dynasty.* YOS, Babylonian Texts 4. New Haven: Yale University Press.

Kramer, Samuel N.

1963 *The Sumerians: Their History, Culture, and Character.* Chicago: University of Chicago Press.

Kraus, F. R.

1958 "Di til.la Sumerische Prozessprotokolle und Verwandtes aus der Zeit der III. Dynastie von Ur." *BO* 15:70–84.

1959–62 "Briefschreibübungen im altbabylonischen Schulunterricht." *JEOL* 6:16–39.

1975–76 "Einführung in die Briefe in altakkadischer Sprache." *JEOL* 24:74–104.

Laessøe, Jørgen

1963 *People of Ancient Assyria: Their Inscriptions and Correspondence.* London: Routledge & Kegan Paul.

Lafont, Bertrand

1985 *Documents administratifs sumériens provenant du site de Tello et conservés au Musée du Louvre.* Paris: Éditions Recherche sur les Civilisations.

1986 "A propos de la ville de Suse et d'un fragment d'enveloppe." *RA* 80:75–76.

1987 "Les deux tablettes néo-sumériennes de Mari." *M.A.R.I.* 5:626–27.

1990 "Nouvelles lettres du temps des rois d'Ur." *RA* 84:165–69.

Lafont, Bertrand and Fatma Yıldız
1989 *Tablettes cunéiformes de Tello au Musée d'Istanbul: Datant de l'époque de la IIIe Dynastie d'Ur, I (ITT II/1,617–1038).* Uitgaven van het Nederlands Historisch-Archeologisch Instituut te Istanbul 65. Leiden: Nederlands Historisch-Archeologisch Instituut te Istanbul.

Lambert, Maurice
1975 "Mesag le prince et Mesag le shabra (la vie économique à l'époque d'Agadé)." *Rivista degli Studi Orientali* 49:159–84.
1979 "Le prince de Suse Ilish-mani, et l'Elam de Naramsin à Ibisîn." *Journal Asiatique* 267:11–40.

Langdon, Stephen H.
1911 *Tablets from the Archives of Drehem.* Paris: Paul Geuthner.

Limet, Henri
1973 *Étude des documents de la période d'Agadé appartenant à l'Université de Liège.* Bibliothèque de la Faculté de Philosophie et Lettres, Fasc. CCVI. Paris: Société d'Edition "Les Belles Lettres."
1976 *Textes sumériens de la IIIe Dynastie d'Ur.* Documents du Proche Orient ancien, Épigraphie 1. Brussels: Musées Royaux d'Art et d'Histoire.

Liverani, Mario
1988 *Antico Oriente: Storia, società, economia.* Rome: Laterza.

Lutz, Henry Frederick
1928 *Sumerian Temple Records of the Late Ur Dynasty.* University of California Publications in Semitic Philology, Volume 9, no. 2, pp. 117–268. Berkeley: University of California Press.

Meek, Theophile James
1935 *Old Akkadian, Sumerian, and Cappadocian Texts from Nuzi.* HSS 10. Excavations at Nuzi 3. Cambridge: Harvard University Press.

Michalowski, Piotr
1976a "Six Neo-Sumerian Letter-Orders." *JCS* 28:161–68.
1976b "The Royal Correspondence of Ur." Diss., Yale University. Ann Arbor: University Microfilms.
1981 "Königsbriefe." *Reallexikon der Assyriologie* 6:51–59.

van de Mieroop, Marc
1984 "Notes on a Sumerian Letter-Order." *OLP* 15:55–58.

Nakahara, Yomokuro
1928 *The Sumerian Tablets in the Imperial University of Kyoto.* Memoirs of the Research Department of the Toyo-Bunko 3. Kyoto: The Toyo-Bunko.

Neumann, Hans
1980 "Ein Ur III-Brief aus der Sammlung des Archäologischen Museums der Martin-Luther-Universität Halle-Wittenberg." *AoF* 7:269–72.

1988 "Der sumerische brief UVB 7, Taf. 23c (W 15966c)." *AoF* 15:209–10.

1992 "Ein Brief an König Šulgi in einer späten Abschrift." *AoF* 19:29–39.

Nies, James B.

1920 *Ur Dynasty Tablets: Texts Chiefly from Tello and Drehem, Written During the Reigns of Dungi, Bur-Sin, Gimil-Sin, and Ibi-Sin.* Assyriologische Bibliothek 25. Leipzig: Hinrichs.

Nikol'skii, M. V.

1915 *Dokumenty khoziaistvennoi otchetnosti drevneishei epokhi Khaldei iz sobraniia N. P. Likchacheva, chast II: Epokha dinastii Agade i epokha dinastii Ura.* Drevnosti Vostochnyja 5. Moscow: Vostochnoia Kommissia Imperatorskago Moskovskago Arkheologicheskago Obshchestva.

Oppenheim, A. Leo

1967 *Letters from Mesopotamia: Official, Business, and Private Letters on Clay Tablets from Two Millennia.* Chicago: University of Chicago Press.

1977 *Ancient Mesopotamia: Portrait of a Dead Civilization.* Revised edition completed by Erica Reiner. Chicago: University of Chicago Press.

Owen, David I.

1971 "Ur III Letter-Orders from Nippur in the University Museum." *Or*NS 40:386–400.

1972 "A Unique Ur III Letter-Order in the University of North Carolina." *JCS* 24:133–34.

1973 "Miscellanea Neo-Sumerica I-III." Pp. 131–37 in *Orient and Occident: Studies Presented to Cyrus H. Gordon on the Occasion of his Sixty-fifth Birthday.* Ed. by Harry H. Hoffner, Jr. AOAT 22. Neukirchen-Vluyn: Neukirchener Verlag.

1975 *The John Frederick Lewis Collection.* MVN 3. Rome: Multigrafia Editrice.

1982a *Neo-Sumerian Archival Texts Primarily from Nippur in the University Museum, The Oriental Institute, and the Iraq Museum.* Winona Lake: Eisenbrauns.

1982b *Selected Ur III Texts in the Harward* [*sic!*]*) Semitic Museum.*MVN 11. Rome: Multigrafia Editrice.

1991 *Neo-Sumerian Texts from American Collections.*MVN 15. Rome: Multigrafia Editrice.

Parr, P. A.

1972 "A Letter of Ur-Lisi, Governor of Umma." *JCS* 24:135–36.

Peat, J.

1976 "A Collection of Ur III Tablets." *JCS* 28:201–26.

Pettinato, Giovanni
1968 "Aggiunte al Corpus di lettere amministrative della terza dinastia di Ur." *Oriens Antiquus* 7:165–79.
1977a *Testi economici di Lagaš del Museo di Istanbul—Parte I: La. 7001–7600.* MVN 6. Rome: Multigrafia Editrice.
1977b "Gli Archivi reali di Tell Mardikh-Ebla: Riflessioni e prospettive." *Rivista Biblica Italiana* 25:225–43.
1980 "Bolletino militare della campagna di Ebla contro la città di Mari." *Oriens Antiquus* 19:231–45.
1991 *Ebla: A New Look at History.* Baltimore: The Johns Hopkins University Press.

Pettinato, Giovanni, and Sergio A. Picchioni
1978 *Testi economici di Lagaš del Museo di Istanbul—Parte II: La. 7601–8200.* MVN 7. Rome: Multigrafia Editrice.

Pettinato, Giovanni, and Hartmut Waetzoldt
1974 *La Collezione Schollmeyer.* MVN 1. Rome: Multigrafia Editrice.
1985 *G. Reisner, Tempelurkunden aus Telloh: Testi.* Studi per il vocabulario Sumerico 1/1. Rome: Il Bagatto.

Platt, James H.
1988 "Notes on Ebla Graphemics." *Vicino Oriente* 7:245–48.

Pohl, A.
1937 *Rechts- und Verwaltungsurkunden der III. Dynastie von Ur.* TMH, Neue Folge 1/2. Leipzig: J. C. Hinrichs.

Powell, M. A.
1989–90 "Maße und Gewichte," *Reallexicon der Assyriologie* 7:457–517.

Reisner, George Andrew
1901 *Tempelurkunden aus Tello.* Berlin: W. Spemann.

Schileico, V. K.
1914–15 "Das sechsseitige Tonprisma Lugal-ušumgal's aus der Sammlung Lichatschew." *Zeitschrift für Assyriologie* 29:78–84.

Seltz, G. J.
1991 "'"Elam" und "Sumer"'—Skizze einer Nachbarschaft nach inschriftlichen Quellen der vorsargonischen Zeit." Pp. 27–43 in *Mésopotamie et Elam: Actes de la XXXVIème Rencontre Assyriologique Internationale, Gand, 10-14 juillet 1989.* Mesopotamian History and Environment, Occasional Publications 1. Ghent: University of Ghent.

Sigrist, Marcel
1983 *Textes économiques néo-sumériens de l'Université de Syracuse.* Paris: Éditions Recherche sur les Civilizations.
1984 *Neo-Sumerian Account Texts in the Horn Archaeological Museum.* Institute of Archaeology Publications, Assyriological Series 4. AUCT 1. Berrien Springs: Andrews University Press.

1988 *Isin Year Names.* Institute of Archaeology Publications, Assyriological Series 2. Berrien Springs: Andrews University Press.

Sigrist, Marcel, and Carney E. S. Gavin

1988 *Neo-Sumerian Account Texts in the Horn Archaeological Museum.* Institute of Archaeology Publications, Assyriological Series 6. AUCT 3. Berrien Springs: Andrews University Press.

Sigrist, Marcel, and Tohru Gomi

1991 *The Comprehensive Catalogue of Published Ur III Texts.* Bethesda: CDL Press.

Simmons, Stephen D.

1978 *Early Old Babylonian Documents.* YOS 14. New Haven: Yale University Press.

Smith, Sidney

1932 "Notes on the Gutian Period." *JRAS* 295–308.

Sollberger, Edmond

1954–56 "Sur la chronologie des rois d'Ur et quelques problèmes connexes." *Archiv für Orientforschung* 17:10–48.

1956a "Selected Texts from American Collections." *JCS* 10:11–31.

1956b *Corpus des inscriptions "royales" présargoniques de Lagaš*. Geneva: E. Droz.

1966 *The Business and Administrative Correspondence under the Kings of Ur.* TCS 1. Locust Valley, NY: J. J. Augustin.

1972 *Pre-Sargonic and Sargonic Economic Texts.* CT 50. London: British Museum.

Speleers, Louis

1925 *Recueil des inscriptions de l'Asie Antérieure des Musées Royaux du Cinquantenaire à Bruxelles: Textes sumériens, babyloniens et assyriens.* Brussels: Vanderpoorten et Co.

Steinkeller, Piotr

1984 "Old Akkadian Miscellanea." *RA* 78:83–88.

1987 "The Foresters of Umma: Toward a Definition of Ur III Labor." Pp. 73–115 in *Labor in the Ancient Near East.* Ed. by Marvin A. Powell. American Oriental Series 68. New Haven: American Oriental Society.

Steinkeller, Piotr, and J. N. Postgate

1992 *Third-Millennium Legal and Administrative Texts in the Iraq Museum, Baghdad.* Mesopotamian Civilizations 4. Winona Lake: Eisenbrauns.

Szlechter, Émile

1963 *Tablettes juridiques et administratives de la IIIe dynastie d'Ur et de la Ire dynastie de Babylone, conservées au Musée de l'Université de Manchester et à Cambridge, au Musée Fitzwilliam, à l'Institut d'Études Orientales et à l'Institut d'Egyptologie.* Paris: Recueil Sirey.

Thureau-Dangin, François
1903 *Recueil de tablettes chaldéennes.* Paris: Ernest Leroux.
1907 "Une incursion élamite en territoire sumérien à l'époque pré-sargonique." *RA* 6:139–42.
1910 *Textes de l'époque d'Agadé (Fouilles d'Ernest de Sarzec en 1894).* ITT 1. Paris: Ernest Leroux.
1926 "Une lettre de l'époque de la dynastie d'Agadé," *RA* 23:23–29.

Touzalin, Maryse
1982 *L'administration palatiale à l'époque de la Troisième Dynastie d'Ur: Textes inédits du musée d'Alep.* Thèse de doctorat de troisième cycle soutenue à l'université de Tours.

Vanstiphout, H. L. J.
1988 "*Mihiltum,* or the Image of Cuneiform Writing." *Visible Religion* 6:152–67.

Veenhof, K. R.
1975–76 "An Old Akkadian Private Letter." *JEOL* 24:105–10.

Volk, Konrad
1992 "Puzur-Mama und die Reise des Königs." *Zeitschrift für Assyriologie* 82:22–29.

Waetzold, Hartmut
1976 "Kollationen zu A. Pohl, Rechts- und Verwaltungsurkunden der III. Dynastie von Ur, TMH Neue Folge 1/2," *Oriens Antiquus* 17:317–28.

Watelin, Louis Charles, and Stephen H. Langdon
1930 *Excavations at Kish: The Herbert Weld (for the University of Oxford) and Field Museum of Natural History (Chicago) Expedition to Mesopotamia, III.* Paris: Paul Geuthner.

Westenholz, Aage
1974 "Old Sumerian and Old Akkadian Texts in the National Museum of Copenhagen." *JCS* 26:71–80.
1984 Review of Foster 1982a. *Archiv für Orientforschung* 31:76–81.
1975 *Early Cuneiform Texts in Jena: Pre-Sargonic and Sargonic Documents from Nippur and Fara in the Hilprecht-Sammlung vorderasiatischer Altertümer Institut für Altertumswissenschaften der Friedrich-Schiller-Universität, Jena.* Det Kongelige Danske Videnskabernes Selskab. Historisk-Filosofiske Skrifter 7, 3. Copenhagen: Munksgaard.

van der Westhuizen, Jasper P.
1989 "Six Old Akkadian Letters." *ASJ* 11:277–84.
1990 "Seven More Old Akkadian Letters." *ASJ* 12:261–69.

Whiting, Robert
1972 "The Dual Personal Pronouns in Akkadian." *JNES* 31:331–37.

Wilcke, Claus
1977 "From Trade to Murder." *JCS* 29:185–86.

1978 "Zur Deutung der SI.BI-Klausel in den spätaltbabylonischen Kaufverträgen aus Nordbabylonien." *Welt des Orients* 9:206–12.

Yang, Zhi

1989 *Sargonic Inscriptions From Adab.* The Institute for the History of Ancient Civilizations Periodic Publications on Ancient Civilizations 1. Changchun: The Institute for the History of Ancient Civilizations.

Yıldız, Fatma, and Tohru Gomi

1988 *Die Puzriš-Dagan-Texte der Istanbuler Archäologischen Museen, Teil II: Nr. 726–1379.* Freiburger Altorientalische Studien 16. Stuttgart: Franz Steiner.

Yıldız, Fatma, Hartmut Waetzoldt, and H. Renner

1988 *Die Umma-Texte aus den Archäologischen Museen zu Istanbul Nr. 1–600.* MVN 14. Rome: Multigrafia Editrice.

Yoshikawa, Mamoru

1984 "Four Sumerian Letter-Orders in Japanese Collections." *ASJ* 6:121–31.

Zettler, Richard L.

1984 "The Genealogy of the House of Ur-Me-me: a Second Look." *Archiv für Orientforschung* 31:1–9.

Glossary

Anshan. A city in southwestern Iran. Modern Tell-i-Malyan.

Apishal. An unidentified city in the Umma region.

Bagara. One of the main temple complexes of the city of Girsu.

Barasiga. A town in the Lagash area.

Barleycorn. A weight measure equal to 1/180 of a shekel; equivalent to 0.046 grams.

Beer-cake. A baked concoction of spices and other materials that was a crucial component in the making of beer.

Bur. An area measure consisting of 18 iku or 3 eshe; roughly equivalent to 16 acres.

"Carp" grain. A designation for a type of grain that is associated with the spring season when the Euphrates river carp leave the river to spawn in the backwaters.

Conscripts. This translates the difficult Sumerian term éren. In the Ur III period these were men who received rations throughout the year, were under the control of a larger state and/or temple organization, and worked their own prebend land in exchange for part-time labor and military service.

Dubura. A hamlet in the Lagash region.

Ekishnugal. The central temple in the city of Ur, dedicated to the moon god Nanna.

Elam. A designation of the geographical area in southwestern Iran, with Susa as its main city.

Eshe. An area measure equal to six iku, or one third of a bur, roughly equivalent to 5.33 acres.

Eshnunna. A major city in the valley of the Diyala river that cuts through the Zagros mountains that separate Mesopotamia from Iran. Modern Tell Asmar.

Gaesh. A town in the vicinity of Ur.

Gatumdug. A goddess worshiped in Girsu.

Girsu. One of the two principal cities of the state or province of Lagash. Modern Tello.

Gishbare. A god worshiped in Girsu.

Guedena. A territory that delimited the border between the cities of Umma and Lagash. Throughout the early third millennium the control over this field was the main pretext for repeated warfare between these two states.

Gurusala. An unidentified place name.

Gutians. A people from the eastern mountains who first appear during the Akkadian period. On the basis of their names and of a few known words, it is assumed that their language was neither Sumerian nor Semitic. Later Mesopotamian historiography assigned to them the fall of Akkad and credited them with hegemony over Sumer for over a century until the rise of the Ur III kingdom. Modern historians view this period as much shorter.

Hamazi. An unidentified city that has been placed in Iran but could just as well be in northern Mesopotamia or Syria.

Harshi. An unidentified city in Iran.

Iku. An area measure equal to one eighteenth of a bur, or one sixth of an eshe, roughly equivalent to 0.89 acres.

Ilaba. The main god of the city of Agade and, with Inanna, patron god of the Sargonic dynasty.

Inanna. Goddess of war and carnal love, she was worshiped in Agade and was one of the two patron deities of the Sargonic kings.

Karhar. An unidentified city in Iran, probably in the Kermanshah valley.

Kibabar. An unidentified city, possibly in the vicinity of Marad, upstream from Girsu.

Kimash. An unidentified city in Iran.

Kish. The main urban center to the north of Sumer, at the modern tells of Ingharra and Uhaimir.

Kisiga. A town in southern Sumer, possibly modern Tell Lahm, south of Ur.

Lagash. One of the two principal cities of the state or province of Lagash. Modern Al Hiba.

lumaḫḫum. A high-ranking priest, often translated "ecstatic."

Mina. A weight measure consisting of 60 shekels, or 180 barleycorns, roughly equivalent to 500 grams.

"Mountain" grain. A very rare designation for grain attested in Early Dynastic, Akkad period, and Ur III sources. It occurs only twice in the Ur III records, in letter no. 176 of this collection and in one other text.

Nanshe. A fish goddess worshiped primarily in the Lagash region.

Ninegala. A goddess.

Ningirsu. Titular god of the city of Girsu.

Ninmar. A goddess worshiped primarily in the Lagash region.

Ninsun. A goddess who married Lugalbanda, a legendary king of the city of Uruk. Their son was Gilgamesh, a semidivine ruler of Uruk who was the main protagonist of numerous literary compositions.

Nippur. One of the most important Sumerian cities. Nippur was the cult center of the god Enlil, the second most important deity of Sumer.

Shara. Titular deity of the city of Umma.

Shekel. A weight measure equal to 1/60 of a mina or 180 barleycorns; equivalent to 8.33 grams.

Simanum. A city in northern Mesopotamia that was allied by diplomatic marriage to the house of Ur.

Simurum. An unidentified Iranian city, possibly to be located on the lower Zab. It was an important strategic center during the Ur III period. Although at one point it was controlled by the Sumerian kings, it was usually in conflict with the central government.

Subartu (Akkadian, **Subir** in Sumerian). A general term for the northern and northeastern areas bordering on the Ur III state. It is less clear what the meaning was in earlier times, although it must have also encompassed northern and northeastern territories.

Talent. A weight measure consisting of sixty minas; roughly equivalent to thirty kilograms.

Tummal. A cult center of the goddess Ninlil, wife of Enlil, located not far from Nippur.

Umma. One of the largest Sumerian cities. Although it has never been officially excavated, thousands of cuneiform tablets were illegally excavated there. Modern Tell Jokha.

Indexes

Numbers refer to numbered texts in this volume.

I. Deities

II. Personal Names

(Male and female are not indicated, since it is often difficult to determine the gender of personal names in these letters.)

III. Places
(Countries, territories, cities, temples, and fields)

IV. Texts Translated